The Grammar Lady

The Grammar Lady

*How to Mind Your Manners
in Print and in Person*

MARY NEWTON BRUDER

A LARK PRODUCTION

New York

Previously published as *Much Ado About a Lot*

Copyright © 2000 Mary Newton Bruder

Library of Congress Cataloging-in-Publication Data

Bruder, Mary Newton
    The grammar lady : how to mind your manners in print and in
person / by Mary Newton Bruder.—1st ed.
        p.   cm.
    ISBN 0-7868-8435-5
    1. English language—Grammar.   2. English language—Errors of
usage.   I. Title.
PE1112.B736   2000
428.2—dc21   99-35897
                                                                  CIP

Book design by Patrice Sheridan

FIRST PAPERBACK EDITION

10 9 8 7 6 5 4 3 2 1

Contents

PART THREE

Have We Lost Our Minds?   **223**

Acknowledgments

This book would not have been possible without the help and support of the readers of my weekly column and the visitors to my Web site. There is a group of Recreational Grammarians on the site who hold the fort when things get very busy, which is most of the time. Two of them, Lee Ellis and John Breen, have contributed in very special ways. Robin Dellabough planted an idea and nursed it to fruition. Jennifer Lang and her colleagues at Hyperion, especially copy editor Saralyn Fosnight and production editor Adrian James, pruned it into the most pleasing book possible.

My grandmother, Hazel Towner Newton, expected us to speak and behave well. My mother, Gertrude Steger Newton, required politeness always. Mary Beth and Charlie provided basic and continuing support. Thank you all.

MNB

Acknowledgments

From Lark Productions:

Thanks to Lisa DiMona and Karen Watts for their careful reading and willingness to have fun with grammar. Thanks to Laura Spinale and Nancy Inglis for additional editorial assistance. Special thanks to Seth Godin, the fairy godfather of this project.

Important Note to Reader

This is not a book on grammar for Ph.D. candidates in English. Heaven help them if they need my help. No, this book comes straight from the front lines, as a response to the real-life everyday questions I have been attempting to answer for the past ten years. It does not include fancy terms such as "pluperfect" and "predicate pronouns as subjunctive complements." (Well, maybe just a few when absolutely necessary.) Rather, I try to make the rules as simple as possible. I even make up new rules as the need arises! That might mean, in some cases, a very strict old-fashioned grammarian would quibble with me. But everyday life, as you probably have noticed, requires common sense, not rules for the sake of rules. Grammar questions arise out of people's experiences; they do not arise in a nice logical order with chapter headings such as "The Subjunctive Mood."

That's why I have organized my book according to the most common situations you may encounter: the office, the classroom, a wedding, a job interview, answering machines, church, the doctor's office, the telephone, E-mail. Instead of finding a chapter on the difference between "that" and "which," I'll lead you through the grammar minefields of, say, a simple telephone call to introduce oneself to a new in-law. During this stroll down the grammar path, we'll naturally run into the difference between "that" and "which." Or perhaps that's when we'll stumble over a stray apostrophe and put it back in its place. Life's an adventure!

And I'd rather split infinitives than split hairs.

PART ONE

✳

Why Grammar Matters

Chapter One

That Wicked Which

You might wonder how I got into the grammar biz and why on earth we even need a Grammar Lady anyway. I thought you'd never ask. . . .

What gets my goat is knowing that the schools don't really know what they're doing about grammar. If the schools had a consistent policy and a reasonable curriculum about what to teach and how and when to teach it, I'd be a happy woman. But starting in the late 1960s and early 1970s, everything had to be *relevant*. You couldn't teach or learn anything just because there was value in it. You had to learn it for a particular purpose. And people no longer saw the purpose in learning grammar, so teachers stopped teaching it, students stopped learning it, and the whole world pretty much went to hell in a handbasket. (Note to self: Check derivation of the expression "went to hell in a handbasket.")

Once I get everyone on the grammar bandwagon, we should be able to settle on some solid educational standards. It's foolish to be teaching grammar past the sixth grade. The basic elements should be taught by the third grade and after that, children should spend their time refining them and learning vocabulary and new, more complex sentence structure. Contrary to the dearly held beliefs of certain teachers, the purpose of grammar is *not* to learn how to diagram a sentence!

Now pay attention, please: The purpose of grammar is to educate us so that we can *communicate* well with all human beings, maybe even with all living things, across all the generations. The way that you communicate with people tells them a lot about you. How you use the tools of good communication, your grammar, gives an impression that you can't erase once it's been given. Grammar even affects romance. I know because my daughter started dating a young man whose use of language was excruciating: a lot of "you know" and "uh" and "ah." He was quite inarticulate. She no longer goes with him. There may be other reasons she's not going with him, but because of my influence over the years, language means a lot to her. I know what you're thinking. I swear I didn't say a word. I have learned when you pick on your daughter's friends, it can blow up in your face, but that story is a whole different book.

For those of you motivated by more mercenary concerns, let me

Readers often ask the pronunciation or meaning of words they find in newspaper or magazine articles. The words are fairly common in writing but absent in everyday speech. I try to represent the pronunciation of the words without using the complicated symbols of the dictionary. I also provide examples of how each word is used in context. These worrisome words are scattered throughout the book, as I didn't want to worry you all at once.

WORRISOME WORD

UNTENABLE (un-TEN-uh-bull) adj. Unable to be defended, indefensible. *The leaks to the press put the president of the company in an untenable position; he had no choice but to resign.*

say that grammar can save money. Just the other day, a caller who was ordering her office letterhead wanted to know how to make the plural of the company name. She said, "The name ends in *sh* and it looks very funny when I put just an *s* on it." I said, "I *think* that's because you need *es*. If it were *dish,* you'd make it *dishes*." "Oh," she said. "It's a good thing I called you. I would have paid a second time to get this letterhead corrected."

Grammar obviously can save time by keeping you out of situations that would later require apologies like the "dishes" mistake. If you can do the thing right the first time, it doesn't have to be done over. One of my Web friends is a director of a private school out in California. He called about a fund-raising letter his board of directors was going to send to potential contributors. It read "It would be real nice if you blah, blah, blah." He had the letters all printed and *then* decided to check with me. I said, "Well, I think it should be *really*." He said, "Oh, dear." He didn't want to embarrass his board, so he had to do the letter all over again.

There are a lot of different reasons for using good grammar as opposed to bad (and not just because bad grammar makes such persons as English teachers and me go absolutely bananas). First, good grammar enhances communication. Not only can bad grammar make it difficult for a particular sentence to be correctly interpreted, but it can also detract from the message by becoming, in itself, a distraction. There is a restaurant where I often go in spite of its list of specials, which I can hardly stand to read since the spelling and

WORRISOME WORD

OMINOUS (AH-mihn-us) adj. Threatening, portending doom. This word is related to the word *omen. The darkening sky and rising wind looked ominous ahead of the approaching storm. There was an ominous sound to the teacher's voice demanding order in the classroom.*

grammar are so terrible. A person who didn't know how good this restaurant's butterscotch pie is might not be so forgiving.

A second reason for using good grammar: People will judge other people on the basis of their grammar—prospective employers, prospective mates, prospective in-laws, and prospective diners, for example.

Third, while good writers often break grammar rules, they do it for a reason; and they do it for a specific effect. If one doesn't know the rules, one does not know when to break them and what effect the breaking of the rule will have on the reader. Like any art or craft (from painting to making furniture), the more one knows about the basics, the better the result will be.

Still, a lot of younger people insist, "It doesn't matter what I sound like because all my friends sound just like me." If they want only to communicate with their friends, I couldn't agree more, it doesn't matter. But it's not their friends who are going to be giving them jobs. They are not necessarily going to ask only their friends for a date.

A young man called this morning about a split infinitive, so I gave him my usual spiel. "You have to consider your audience," I said, "when deciding whether or not you want to split this infinitive." He said, "I'm writing my application for Harvard Law School." I took a deep breath, counted to ten, and said, "I don't think you ought to split the infinitive. Any infinitive."

This matter of correctness versus formality is endlessly fascinating because there are certain things that are correct in one context but overly formal or stuffy in another. When I taught at the University of Pittsburgh, we moved our offices frequently. One moving day, the chairman of the department, an older man with white hair and a beard, picked up a box of books. The bottom fell out, and the books scattered all over the floor. He looked at the books and said, "Oh, my." Well, the workmen who were helping us move thought this was howlingly funny.

He could have gotten away with "Damn it" or some other mild expletive, but "Oh, my" just threw those workmen into a tizzy. They went around all the rest of the afternoon mimicking him.

A woman in Indiana calls me regularly to complain about her daughter's sixth-grade teacher. The daughter brings home her assignments; the mother helps her; then the teacher says they're wrong. The teacher doesn't have a clue; the woman is almost always right. She worries that her daughter won't learn what needs to be learned because her teacher is an idiot. So she goes to the teacher and raises her voice. Shouting seems to be the only way the mother gets any results, but it's not exactly good manners.

I learned my grammar manners mostly at home. The biggest influence on my language development was not school; it was my grandmother. We used to have those traditional Sunday dinners where everybody came and sat around Grandma's table and discussed the topic of the week. It was shortly after World War II, and my mother worked in my father's machine shop so I went a lot of places with my grandmother and her great friend. They belonged to a book club and I got to hear the ladies discuss the books. Hearing good grammar being spoken is one of the most effective ways for anyone to absorb it. I have been drawn to grammar ever since those early days.

I guess you could say I have a grammar thumb.

Oh, one more thing. I do need to explain a few guidelines before we begin. I'm not called the Grammar *Lady* for just any old reason. While I relish high-minded debate, I shy away from unpleasant confrontations. So in the event you may not agree with some of my grammar decrees, that is all very well—as long as you disagree in

❋**Goofy Goof:** Has anyone ever paid attention to the warning on the outside rearview mirror on automobiles? "Objects in mirror are closer than they appear." There are no objects in the mirror. It should be something like "Objects are closer than they appear in the mirror."

the privacy of your own home. I beseech you not to attack me, call me, or otherwise draw me into an unladylike tiff. I stand for helpful grammar and grammar that helps.

(By the way, the best guess about "going to hell in a handbasket" comes from the days of blasting through the mountains for the railroad line. Chinese laborers, being lighter than the other workers, were lowered over the cliffs in baskets to set the charges. If the dynamite went off before the basket could be hauled back up . . . you get the picture.)

MARY'S BEE

Here's the first spelling test in the book, so it's not very hard. I didn't want you to be discouraged. The definition of the word is first, followed by several choices of spelling. Try to do it without looking in the dictionary. Then check the pronunciation and correct spelling on pages 257–59. I know you won't peek. What fun would that be?

1. Light umbrella to protect from the sun.
    parasall / parasol / parasole

2. Device for showing changing patterns.
    kaleidoscope / kelaidoscope / kalleidoscope

3. Photographers who pursue famous people.
    paparazi / papparazzi / paparazzi

4. Light golden horse with nearly white mane and tail.
    palimino / palomino / pallimino

5. Harsh, unpleasant sound.
   cacophany / cacophony / caccophony

6. To fawn.
   kowtow / kautow / kowtau

7. Dessert topping.
   maringue / marang / meringue

8. Upholstered seat along a wall.
   banquette / bankette / bancquette

9. Casino employee who collects and pays off debts.
   croopier / croupie / croupier

10. Bandage to stop bleeding.
    turniquette / tourniquet / tourniquette

11. Club used by police.
    truncheon / trunchian / trunchen

12. Petty, trivial.
    pickeyune / picayune / piccayune

13. Fit of rage or hysteria.
    conniption / caniption / coniption

14. Triangle with two equal sides.
    isoceles / issoceles / isosceles

15. System of writing for the blind.
    breille / brail / braille

16. Encoding.
incryption / encription / encryption

17. Ceremonial greeting in the Middle East.
salaam / saalam / salahm

18. Confuse.
discumbobulate / discombbulate / discombobulate

19. Shaky, run down.
rickitty / rickety / ricketty

20. A shape like the Washington Monument.
obelisk / obelisque / obbelisk

TYPO OF THE WEAK

A loyal recreational grammarian and friend, John Breen, has been helping me produce Typos of the Weak for some time. Here is John's inimitable introduction to these bloopers:

The Typos of the Weak that follow and that are printed throughout the rest of the book did not get here by accident. Well, they did, of course; they all started as accidents. But once I received and reviewed them, they had to withstand a rigorous scrutiny to ensure that they met *one* of the criteria listed below.

Overall, a Typo of the Weak *must* be a perfectly legitimate word that became another perfectly legitimate word spell-check-proofed. Spell-check software (motto: We Check Every Word Except Context, Or Your Monkey Back) must have reviewed and saluted the word: Pass on through, brother; you're cool! In the process, the new word has become hopelessly, totally, hilariously (and, yes, embarrassingly) out of context.

A Typo of the Weak contains only one of the following:

(1) the accidental omission of only one letter (ex: brain becomes rain);

(2) the accidental addition of only one letter (ex: rain becomes brain);

(3) the accidental replacement of only one letter by another *in its place* (ex: not becomes now. Imagine a Nuclear Reactor User Manual: You must noW activate the atomic vaporizer. Kablooie!! Not a happy thought.)

(4) the accidental twisting of two adjacent letters (twist becomes twits—somewhat rare);

(5) the accidental dividing of a word, i.e., a space between one word that produces, therefore, two words (ex: pantry becomes pan try—If it's not in the pan try the refrigerator. . . . atrophy / a trophy—ex: A trophy was discovered in the patient's left hand.) Quite rare.

(6) likewise, the accidental pushing together of two adjacent, separate words to form one (ex: Atrophy was presented to the muscle-bound wrestler.) Quite rare. I haven't seen one yet, but they're out there, and some informant will come through for us someday.

Anything more sophisticated (a) is not really fair and doesn't technically qualify as a true spell-check-proof finger-fumble typo

RESOLUTE (rez-oh-LUTE) adj. Firmly resolved or determined. *We must be resolute in our efforts to get "I" and "me" used correctly.*

and (b) probably belongs in a Freudian Slip or some such category. Example: disparate becomes desperate, in which two nonadjacent letters are affected. This is a stretch and looks contrived. What don't count for our purposes, however, are sentences (not typos) written like the posthoneymoon hubby's. Out of town on a business trip, he enthusiastically sent his new bride a postcard: The scenery is here; wish you were beautiful! While hilarious (to us, rest his soul), it's not Typo of the Weak material for the reasons stated above.

Our sole mission is to emphasize, humorously yet poignantly, the importance of the human editor, who understands context and will never be replaced by computers.

Typo of the Weak

From a would-be government contractor proposal's Corporate Qualifications section to provide an agency with all the latest bells-and-whistles-laden hardware. And we thought the mouse was the latest innovation.

We continually provide our clients with state-of-the-rat hardware.

Typo of the Weak

From a would-be government contractor proposal's Management section, it obviously suggests that there's a whole lot of work involved here.

We have ascertained that the project will require 66 man-moths of experience.

Typo of the Weak

From a would-be government contractor's proposal account of being cited by a very high-level navy official, this brings new meaning to the term "pocket battleship."

[Flinkets, Inc.] received an award of excellence from the Thief of Naval Operations.

Typo of the Weak

From a would-be government contractor's proposal. We'll duly deposit this one in our Naval Academy Midshipmen Looking for Summer Lawn Care Work file.

Our goat is total customer satisfaction.

Chapter Two

Me, Myself, and I

Not long ago a student logged on to my Web site and asked, "How does one get the title Grammar Lady? Was it given or is it a name you gave yourself?" It seems the class was having a discussion about this, but did you note the form of the question? How does "one"??? I was so impressed I confessed that I had "borrowed" it from the *Saturday Night Live* character "The Church Lady."

When I first started the Grammar Hotline in Pittsburgh, circa 1986, it was for the purpose of generating publicity for a literacy organization. There were few calls at first, and the operation was somewhat haphazard because of my teaching load at the University of Pittsburgh.

Because of my interests in language and research, I started to jot down the questions. Imagine my surprise when the same questions kept recurring. Over the first few years I developed a set of bulletins to cover the most frequently asked queries about commas, apostrophes, affect/effect, lay/lie, spelling rules, irregular verbs—elements of language possessed by anyone graduating from any American elementary school through the 1950s. Since most of the callers were adults calling from business offices and were therefore professionals or people working for professionals, I began to be suspicious that some sea change had occurred in the public schools since I had last noticed. This suspicion was amplified when I realized that many of the callers were older women, secretaries trying to settle arguments with their younger bosses. (The secretaries were almost invariably correct—they had gone to school when learning to spell and punctuate correctly was not optional.)

I closed the hotline down when I took my summer vacation at our cabin without electricity in the Finger Lakes region of upstate New York. This was before the ubiquitous cellular phone. (Notice how it's gotten shortened to cell phone?) There was a lot of complaining from people who'd come to rely on the hotline service, so I tried to keep it going the next summer by forwarding the calls to the Linguistics Department where I had taught. That didn't work out so well because callers complained that the questions weren't answered to their satisfaction. (I never asked, but I suspect graduate students who had the same knowledge level as the bosses being corrected by their secretaries were giving out the answers.)

When I decided to go national in 1997 with a Web site and an 800 number, the situation in Pittsburgh turned out to be the tip of the proverbial iceberg. From all over the country came a litany of calls, especially from California for some odd reason. Have the schools in California taken the lead yet again and abolished the English language from school curricula? Or maybe the earthquakes rattled people's brains as well as the buildings and their grammar was a major casualty. I'm sure if we work at it, we can find a way to blame El Niño.

After a year of national exposure, I am a woman on a mission—a mission to address the usage of English grammar, to restore its

***

❋**Goofy Goof:** I overheard someone shouting to a friend in (a big department store) recently: "I AIN'T NEVER TELLING YOUSE NOTHING NO MORE!"

teaching in a reasonable way to the public schools, and to raise awareness in general about the disreputable state of our national, if unofficial, language. Finally, I want to persuade everyone who reads this book that language, grammar and all, can be a whole lot of fun. We just have to lighten up a little.

I do not believe in the causes of those who seek to preserve forever a "pure" form of the language, nor do I think it possible to stop language change. Living languages change over time, as do all living things. (If you want a pure, unchanging language, try Latin or Esperanto.) What we are in the midst of, however, is approaching anarchy. Have you talked to any of those young Valley Girl types who end every statement with a rising inflection so you can't tell if they are asking a question: "My name is Mary?" "I need some help?" Yes, you do, dear, but not the kind you think. A regular on the site has gleaned these invented words from her consulting business. Instivingual = an individual so large and imposing as to become an institution. Advision = the act of advising: When you advise someone, you have committed advision. Unless the brakes are applied to the chaos, we will lose the mutual comprehensibility that glues us to the rest of the English-speaking world.

SPOKEN VERSUS WRITTEN LANGUAGE

It seems rather obvious to say that spoken language is different from written language in substantial ways, but a lot of people don't want to believe it. These are the folks who want us all to sound like Miss Fidditch all the time, even to the police officer who pulls us over for a speeding violation with "Oh, yes, Officer. And how may I help you this fine day?" People who sound like this no matter what the situation are courting a straitjacket.

There is a range of spoken styles of language, described by an old-fashioned linguist by the name of Martin Joos (*The Five Clocks*), that most people switch among rather effortlessly. There is a style used at home and among very close friends: *Intimate*. Don't get the wrong idea, we're not talking about "pillow talk," but a style of language characterized by sentence fragments, missing helping verbs, renewed conversations after hours of interval, a style totally incomprehensible to outsiders.

When I formally retired from teaching (informally I will never retire), it meant that my husband, a self-employed business owner, and I would both be working out of our residence. My advice to any long-marrieds who are contemplating such a move is to give it more contemplation than we did. Charlie was not pleased to have to change out of his gym clothes when the *USA Today* photographer showed up. And how could I have known we played different solitaire games on my computer, and he always left his on the screen? Or that he had the TV on as background whereas I needed a radio or nothing.

When there is an official "going to work" routine, the speech events are well set: getting up, leaving, coming home at the end of day, dinner, evening routines. The information exchanged is predictable: "What's for dinner?" "How was your day," etc. Pretty bland stuff all in all. (Not the stuff for soap opera.)

But when whole days have to be negotiated, "Men are from GM and women are from Ford" takes on a different meaning altogether. Suffice it to say we have survived the new relationship for a year and a half, so I think we're okay; but it has given me many insights into communication on this level.

WORRISOME WORD

EFFULGENT (ih-FULL-jent) adj. Shining brilliantly; radiant. *The crystals of the antique chandelier were effulgent in the candlelit room.*

Here is a sample of intimate dialogue—hope it doesn't give this style a bad name.

CHARLIE: Gotta get a door for the office. Wanna get out of the house?

ME: Too much work. H'll go. (H refers to the dog. He takes dog and leaves.)

(Later)

ME: Well?

CHARLIE: Two hundred seventy-nine and a three-week delivery.

ME: A lotta rats can get in by then.

CHARLIE: Yeah. I'll try the other one.

ME: Where's that?

CHARLIE: By where Phyllis lives.

ME: Way down there?

CHARLIE: The only place left.

This totally banal conversation went on the better part of a day and was interspersed with similar snippets dealing with a computer problem. Note the lack of "pleasantries," transitions, and complete sentences, and the presence of inside references. The context of our situation filled in all the spaces for both of us, but analysis of a taped transcript would have most psychologists shaking their heads at these people's problems with "interactive communication."

Even other family members can be baffled by this kind of intimacy. My husband and I had been debating the purchase of a new computer system over six months. Our college-age daughter accompanied us on numerous futile visits to computer stores. During the final one, a repeat of the previous half-dozen, she wandered off to a pet store. When she returned twenty minutes later, we were signing the bill of sale. She threw up her hands: "I don't get this! You dither for months and I'm gone for twenty minutes and you make up your minds just like that!" While she was gone we had gotten the information that there was a special sale, and there was only one computer left. The two facts were all we needed to finish the purchase of this computer. Even our own daughter was out of the loop.

The second speaking style is called *Informal*; it's what friends and long-term colleagues use together. This became crystal clear when one of my English as a Second Language (ESL) students said to me one day after class, "How come I can understand you perfectly in class, but don't understand a word when you talk to the other teachers?" Teachers, and ESL teachers especially, monitor their speech very carefully to maximize communication with a class of mixed native languages where English is the only choice. Outside of class, teachers revert to a collegial informal language of shared tasks and knowledge. This language is characterized by wanna, gotta, gonna, and is generally faster than the careful "teacher speak."

When we first moved to Pittsburgh, I discovered a local diner with really good food and cheap prices. On one occasion the local letter carrier was engaged in conversation with the waitress. I could tell by the body language that they were friends and could hear their voices quite clearly. By the intonation I knew they were speaking English, but because of the combination of the Pittsburgh regional dialect and the informal style they were using, I could not decipher a single word. I felt just like my ESL students.

WORRISOME WORD

EPIGRAM (EH-pih-gram) n. A terse, witty saying or poem. John Barrymore once said, "The way to fight a woman is with your hat. Grab it and run." Here's one by Ogden Nash: "Children aren't happy with nothing to ignore, And that's what parents were created for."

The third speaking style is called *consultative*, the language used when talking to strangers—getting the time on a street corner, directions to a destination, that kind of thing. The contact is limited and follows a fairly strict formula, but since the object is to get information, you want to speak clearly and present the best face you can.

On a recent trip to Boston we became hopelessly lost trying to find "Old Ironsides." My husband pulled up to a young man and instructed me to ask him. Well, let me tell you there is a knack to choosing consultants in strange places. The one we chose—in Boston, remember—was wearing a University of Michigan sweatshirt and turned out to be a native speaker of Spanish. (We couldn't tell about the language until he answered, but we could have guessed from the shirt that he was from out of town.) He thought we wanted the post office and promptly provided explicit directions that probably would have landed us on Cape Cod. We finally found a toll booth operator—they know everything, as do mail carriers and people in firehouses. There, that's the kind of little gem of a tip I'm going to throw in throughout the book. So stay on your reading toes and pay attention. No skipping.

A word of advice: when asked to give directions to strangers visiting in your hometown, if you don't know the way, say so; and give the tourists a break. Making up bogus directions just gets them more lost, and they will conclude that the natives are as stupid as you think the visitors are for not being able to find their way around your perfectly marked town. The Chamber of Commerce should

WORRISOME WORD

CENSURE (SEN-shur) n. A strong expression of disapproval; v. to criticize in a harsh manner. *The newspaper editorials were unanimous in their censure of the proposed tax increase. The Senate censured its members who were involved in the scandal.*

give "polite lessons" just prior to the tourist season in each area. I bet it would increase tourist dollars enormously.

The fourth speaking style is heard from the lectern, the political stump, and the pulpit: *formal*. It is characterized by long Latinate and Greek words, complex and compound sentences, and a format of introduction, central points, and conclusion. Discussions following these events tend to use the same language style, with everyone on his or her best language behavior. People learn this form of speech as adults, often in their chosen academic field. Most undergraduates learn to decipher and comprehend this style, often without learning to create it themselves.

Any presidential inaugural comes to mind, as does Martin Luther King's famous "I have a dream" speech.

WRITING STYLES

For the most part, until the advent of the Internet, personal styles were found in diaries and friendly letters that people used regularly for correspondence. My mother has saved the weekly letters I sent home during my undergraduate days. Maybe someday I will have the courage to reread them—maybe not. Young people made fools of themselves regularly in those days, and I probably told Mom and Dad some pretty tall tales.

The formal written style that used to be taught in school is the nearest to the formal speaking style, and therefore easiest to learn by people who grow up speaking standard English. In interviews, I often tell talk show hosts that the best present parents can give their children is to speak standard English in the home. That way, in order to become a good writer, all the child has to learn are the fundamentals peculiar to writing: parallel structure, rhetorical forms, organization of ideas, and so forth.

When we think about it, we can see that children come to school at the age of five or six with most of their spoken language patterns set, including regional dialects. From then until about puberty, when the peer group takes on more importance, parental input is still more powerful than teacher-child interactions in school, so the child who arrives speaking standard English will not suffer too much. The school is instrumental when the child arrives speaking nonstandard English. I do not believe the school has the responsibility to teach morals and values, or even driver training, but I do think schools should teach reading, writing, and standard English.

Oh, I know someone out there is going to ask me to define standard English, and in my heart of hearts, I wish we could all sound like Walter Cronkite. But I know that's a lost dream. We know the things nonstandard English includes: he don't know; it ain't late; he has went; I been. It is not hard for teachers to correct young children who use these patterns, but the teachers have to care and the parents have to insist that they do. In an earlier age, immigrants made certain that their children learned English in school, even if it meant loss of their native language. They understood that language was the key to their children's success in this country. The schools participated enthusiastically in the transformation.

Proper use of English is still a key to success in many areas of life, but most of the schoolchildren today are native speakers of

---

WORRISOME WORD

RENEGE (rih-NIHG/NEHG) v. To go back on one's word. *After the long peace process, each side reneged on its promises within days. Note:* The word is commonly used when playing card games in which one must follow suit when able. If a player breaks this rule, he is said to have reneged.

some sort of English. Since it's deemed dangerous to self-esteem to point out errors, the students who don't use the language correctly don't get much help.

As you probably can guess, I will have more to say about language lessons in schools later on, but suffice it to say for now that today no one comes to school knowing how to write standard formal English. That must be taught in school to all comers.

This book will address many of the questions that have come (over and over and over) to the attention of the Grammar Lady. They will be addressed in a social context because the way we use language depends in part on where we are and who is around. Splitting infinitives is fine for Trekkies (to boldly go where no one . . .), but I wouldn't recommend it in an application letter to graduate school.

That old cliché of the 1980s—we only get one chance to make a first impression—is true in our speech, too. In the words of Nancy Kukura, a teacher from Massachusetts and Grammar Lady fan, "The words that come out of our mouths are like the clothes we wear on our backs. We wouldn't go to the office in tattered, dirty clothes; why should the things we say be ragged and rough?"

No matter what, grammar matters.

MARY'S BEE

Here are more words that are often misspelled. Correct the ones that are spelled incorrectly. (To keep you on your bees' knees, some are correct, and are marked as such with the answers.)

1. abundent
2. division
3. expensive

4. dilema
5. hospitel
6. percieve
7. preceed
8. succede
9. sponsor
10. souvenir

Typo of the Weak

From a government contractor's proposal. We know that cattle and kings have taken up temporary residence in at least one, but a Q.A. shop?

This document has been quality-assured by the Documentation Manger.

Typo of the Weak

From a government contractor proposal's personnel qualifications section, it brings new meaning to the term "high technology."

He has experience in retrieval, storing, and snorting procedures.

Typo of the Weak

From a corporate flyer giving directions to the annual company picnic. In God we trust, but what if we were lifelong Democrats?

Immediately after existing, get into the far right lane.

Typo of the Weak

From a Big Apple corporation's puff piece come prime, high-level candidates for Macy's Thanksgiving parade; we wonder if they provide their own rope too.

We have expanded our officers in New York City.

PART TWO

When, Where, and to Whom Grammar Matters

Chapter Three

That's Entertainment

The entertainment industry has always influenced American culture, sometimes as a mirror, at other times leading the way. The advent of radio broadcasting united Americans in ways previously unknown. The stereotypical image of the nuclear family huddled before the radio, listening to F.D.R.'s latest update on the movement of troops during World War II, comes close to hitting the mark. The glamorous image of big-screen smokers—Bette Davis, Joan Crawford, and their ilk—encouraged many of us to take up the habit.

A character on a 1940s sitcom regularly used the word "irregardless." I still get calls from people asking whether "irregardless" is a word. (It is not.) The effect of radio, television, and motion pictures on the language is perhaps subtle, but it's there.

For example, a reader wrote, "A few years back I worked with some people from the South who used an expression new to me. I don't even know how to spell it. It's a verb, pronounced "BOE (rhymes with toe) guard," and seems to mean to push or shove, as in 'He boeguarded his way past me.' Are you familiar with it?" I wasn't. So I put the questions to my readers. I received a record number of calls. Some people, noting that my first correspondent had heard Southerners use the phrase, suggested its origins might sit with Pierre Gustave Beauregard, the Confederate general who directed the bombardment of Fort Sumter. As fans of *Casablanca, The Maltese Falcon,* and *The African Queen* have probably already guessed, that suggestion was wrong.

The expression reported as "boeguard" is actually a verb: "to Bogart." It means to get one's way by intimidation, à la everyone's favorite 1940s tough guy. Use of Humphrey's last name as a verb appeared in black dialect of the 1940s. The 1969 movie *Easy Rider* featured a song called "Don't Bogart Me." It involved two friends sharing—or not sharing—a joint. The verb "to Bogart" thus passed into hippie slang with a new meaning: "to hog," especially to hog a certain type of cigarette. Today, according to my younger callers, the verb can mean either "to hog" or "to intimidate." They provide me with examples such as "He bogarted that book I wanted," and "They bogarted their way in front of me."

DON'T BELIEVE EVERYTHING YOU HEAR IN THE THEATER

Much of what comes to us, languagewise, via the movies is faddish and quick to disappear. As an example, take *Wayne's World.* Oh please, please take *Wayne's World.*

"Is there a new grammar pattern?" a correspondent asked. "I've even seen this in print. There's a sentence, then a dash, and then the word *not.* For example, 'That is my final word—not!!' I know that in some other languages, there are negative elements added to the end of a sentence, but I never heard of it in English."

I responded that I thought this use of the word *not* was a current language fad, but I couldn't be sure because my expert wasn't available at the moment. (My teenage daughter was out with her friends.) Luckily, a reader filled in the terrible void: "It was made popular, I think, by the movie *Wayne's World*. The speaker says something pretty outrageous, then pauses for a few seconds, then says 'not.' It substitutes for sarcasm, which people don't know how to do any more. A few years ago when I was in school, we used the word *psych* instead. We'd say something ridiculous, look at the shocked face of an unsuspecting classmate, then shout 'Psych!' meaning, 'I psyched you out.' "

People who continue to use faddish speech after it has passed from common use mark themselves as coming from a certain generation. People my age, for example, say "groovy" when they mean "cool." Saying "groovy" is way uncool, my daughter tells me. In my opinion, Congress should pass a law mandating that Hollywood produce a movie like *Clueless* every ten years or so. That way we geezers can, like, totally relate to the younger folks who volunteer to wheel us around.

Most of these faddish figures of speech do not, thank goodness, make their way into print. Still, since parents and teachers have, over the last few decades, seemed to have completely stopped monitoring their young charges' speech, a plethora of grown-up professional types now employ extremely bad grammar.

My readers tell me all about it.

"There is a morning network TV host who announces breaks in the program by saying 'We're back in a moment . . .' " a reader wrote. "I've been out of school a long time, but is this a new grammatical construction that I've missed? Shouldn't he say something like 'We will be back in a moment. . . .'?" Of course he should, I replied. There are some cases when the present tense is used for future actions, such as "The plane gets in at ten." But the example cited above just sounds wrong. And now I hear Alex Trebek saying it on *Jeopardy!* Fie and for shame, Mr. Trebek!

A caller commented that on a recent talk show the guest, a "doctor" of something or other, was advocating that teachers be paid on a commission basis. He used the phrase "because whomever is being evaluated . . ." My caller couldn't understand how someone who can't use the English language properly is given air time as an authority on education. I agreed wholeheartedly and urged my correspondent to write an indignant note to the host. He promised he would. (Note to self: Maybe I should develop a line of generic indignant notes and market them through the Web site. Grammar Lady vs. Hallmark.)

People who have the power to influence language use and do so in a negative way need to be reminded of the responsibility that goes with such power. The schools are excoriated daily for their failure to educate our young people. But think about it: Kids spend thirty to forty hours a week in school. During the rest of their waking hours (conservatively seventy) they are exposed in one way or other to a huge, monolithic entertainment culture that is mostly about making a buck, ungrammatically for the most part. I have not commented on all the language use of these pop culture icons without awareness of the consequences. I know that invitations to appear on certain talk shows will not be forthcoming. Frankly, my dears, I don't give a . . .

TV OR NOT TV

I sometimes lose heart watching television. I too often hear the cream of our society making grammatical errors.

Microsoft guru Bill Gates once told a television reporter, "My parents provided a good childhood for my sister and I." Clearly, the years did not include the study of parts of speech. If they had, he

✳**Goofy Goof:** Our local paper had the past tense of the verb "fling" as flang.

would have known that the correct use is "my sister and me." Instead, the young Master Gates merely invented that pesky Windows operating system, earning a paltry gazillion or two in the process. In all seriousness, Gates is the type of public figure who can influence patterns of speech. It was hard for me to listen to him mutilate the language—especially because this interview centered on the use of computers in schools.

I eventually got so fed up with the misuse of the pronouns "I," "me," and "myself" that I started a national campaign to correct the perpetrators. We sent out notes and had a little success. This letter was sent to radio producers, TV producers, advertisers, and anyone else the Grammar Lady multitudes caught in I/me/myself errors.

The Grammar Lady
Mary Newton Bruder
264 Washington Road
Pittsburgh, PA 15216

HELP STOP THE ABUSE OF
PERSONAL PRONOUNS

The abuse of all the personal pronouns, but particularly "I" and "me," has gotten out of hand.

For example, during one infamous *X-Files* episode, this bit of dialogue occurred:

SCULLY: Do you have a warrant for X's arrest? Let Mulder and I serve it. [Let I serve it?!]

In a current allergy-medicine commercial, a young woman says: "We go fishing every year, just Dad and me." [Dad and me go fishing every year?]

The boomers who write the TV scripts regularly make these

errors; Bill Gates did it in a national interview. So did Bill Clinton. If we don't stop it now, this travesty will become part of the standard language.

If that happens, there will be yet one more exception to learn, heaven forbid.

New (if we don't stop this) Rule: When there is only one person following the preposition use me, us, him, her, or them. (They waited for me.) *But* when two people follow a preposition, use I, we, he, she, or they. (They waited for John and I.)

Wrong	*Correct*
between you and I	between you and me
He can *go* with Bill and I.	He can go with Bill and me.
Me and Dad go to the . . .	Dad and I go to the . . .
You and her should be . . .	You and she should be . . .

YOUR INFRACTION: (Here, the Grammar Lady kindly noted where the addressee had messed up.) The _____ publication in March/April 1997 p. 66, printed the phrase: "Where does this leave you and I?"

TRICK: Mentally remove the word before "and," then listen to the sentence. (Where does this leave I? *No.* Where does this leave me? *Yes.* Where does this leave you and me?) You'll know immediately which is right. Do this a few times, and you'll get it right every time thereafter. Think before you commit pronoun abuse again.

Yours, for better grammar,
Mary Newton Bruder
The Grammar Lady

The misuse of pronouns has grown so common that some people now wonder whether the language has changed to accommodate them. One caller told me, "I am appalled by the misuse of 'me' and 'I' by television announcers and artists. Even Angela Lansbury, in *Murder, She Wrote*, used '*I*' for the objective case. Has this become acceptable?" It has not, and it is my fervent hope that it never will. The problem is, our "ears" have changed. People misuse pronouns so often that the misuses are beginning to sound all right to us.

An outraged reader in Pittsburgh complained about a Barnes & Noble radio ad in which a woman shopper concluded her buying spree by saying, "Now, something for his father and I." My reader called the local store to complain about the mistake, but that outlet referred her to Barnes & Noble corporate offices in New York. She followed through—incurring the cost of a long-distance phone call—and a few weeks later the ad was corrected. One victory for the little guys.

PBS airs an educational children's show (mark me, readers, *children's* show) called *Where in the World Is Carmen Sandiego?* It helps teach geography. The host used to preface the program's last segment with the phrase "It's time for you and I to go after . . ." I mentioned this mistake in my newspaper column and, olé, a few episodes later the host announced "It's time for us to go . . ."

These types of mistakes have become so prevalent that people actually ask me, "Is it ever correct to use the pronoun 'me' first, as in 'me and John'? I hear it all the time on TV." If enough people call and threaten to push the Off switch, the media authorities will

WORRISOME WORD

DEIFY (DEE-ih-fye) v. To make a god of; to exalt to the rank of a deity. *Fans whose teams go to the Super Bowl often deify the players and everyone connected with the team. Go Steelers!*

get the message soon enough. Good heavens, what a rant! Being an item on the new *Hollywood Squares* must have gone to my head.

Sad, but true. Of course, this sentence structure is never correct. It sounds self-centered, not to say juvenile and uneducated. Maybe we'll restart this campaign.

AN ODE TO APOSTROPHES

The quickest way to get my dander up is to send me a clipping from an otherwise reputable newspaper with the word *it's* misused in a headline! Will you just look at this:

> USA Confirms That Seinfeld Is It's Favorite Show.
> —*USA Today*

If there were an award for "most common yet easy to avoid mistake," *its* would certainly win. Using *it's* when you mean *its* telegraphs your carelessness. They're so easy to keep straight, for heaven's sake.

Don't be afraid of apostrophes. There is one simple rule to memorize, no judgment calls, no need for an expert. Remember:

It's means *it is*.
   It's time to leave.
   Don't touch that, it's mine.
   Chocolate? It's my favorite!

Its is the possessive.
   The cat cut its paw.
   The town honored its mayor.
   Its point was too dull to cut the mustard.

How to keep them straight? Pretend the apostrophe is the letter *i.* After all, it even looks a little like an *i.*

Thus, it's becomes it is. Whenever you see an apostrophe in the word *it's,* just replace it with an *i* and see if the sentence still makes sense. If there is no apostrophe, you have to remember you're talking about ownership. So, in our infamous *USA Today* headline, all the editor had to do was follow the apostrophe = i rule to discover his mistake.

"USA Confirms That Seinfeld Is It Is Favorite Show" makes no sense at all, now does it?

Speaking of making no sense, right now it's pouring down rain and there's a man across the street washing his driveway.

POLITICS AND GRAMMAR: STRANGE BEDFELLOWS

One correspondent wrote to complain, "I'm so sick of hearing these presidential candidates misuse pronouns. A letter to the editor appearing in a national newspaper asks voters to 'Vote for the First Candidate Who Says, "Between Him and Me." ' What do you think?" I thought the suggestion worthy of high praise, especially after listening to Jack Kemp. Running for vice president in the 1996 elections, Mr. Kemp kept saying "Bob Dole and myself don't see Bill Clinton and Al Gore as the enemies." This use of "myself" where "I" should be annoyed me. But Kemp only followed his boss's lead.

President George Bush campaigned for reelection with the slogan "Who Do You Trust?" I, most emphatically, cannot trust a well-educated man who makes such a grammatical error. During the 1992 campaign, Democrats fared little better, grammarwise. Bill Clinton asked the populace to "Elect Al Gore and I!"

Rule: Keep in mind that *who/whom* is a pair of pronouns just like he/him, she/her, they/them. If you would use he/she (they), use *who*; if you would use him/her (them), use *whom*.

Pronouns used as the subject	Pronouns used as the object of a sentence or a preposition
who	whom
I	me
we	us
you	you
he	him
she	her
they	them

When the words are used to connect sentences, the procedure is the same.

"The new employee who/whom I met today came from New York." Which pronoun should the speaker use? Since he means, "I met him today," the word *whom* is the right choice. "Whom" is the object in the clause "whom I met."

"Does anyone know who/whom the new boss is?" Since "she is the new boss," the speaker should use the word *who*.

In complicated sentences the who/whom pronoun seems to fulfill both the subject and object functions. "I can't make a decision about who/whom has influenced me the most." It's the object of the preposition "about" but the subject of the verb "has influenced." When this happens, the subject wins: Use *who*.

UNFIT TO PRINT

"If it's written down, it must be true." That is some Americans' perception of what they read in the print media. Unfortunately, the grammatical errors that slip into printed matter gain a respect not accorded to mistakes uttered in the spoken word.

Half my callers ring up to complain about things they see in print. I think computerized spelling-and-grammar-checking programs cause much of the problem. Take a gander at the following flagrant fouls.

Subjunctive

Tom Clancy's 1998 *Op-Center: Balance of Power* contains more than a dozen errors with the "If I were/was" (subjunctive/conditional) structure. It seems that when a sentence has the word *if* and a part of the verb to "be," it automatically becomes "were." If a bestselling author and his publisher are having trouble with these, what do the normal folk do? Clancy is old enough to have learned in school that when the "if" is contrary to fact, it takes this special structure, the subjunctive. "If I were in Paris, I would have lunch in a café." But when the "if" clause *is* possible or means *whether*, the regular verb is fine. "If I was late, please excuse me. I don't know if he was late." The problem with such a seemingly inconsequential thing is that it changes the meaning of the passage and makes the reader confused about what is actually happening. But the real damage here is the insult to the readers' intelligence. If the author can't get the language right, I don't have to buy any more of his books. In fact, I doubt Tom will notice his royalty check is a few dollars less.

There are two common uses of this little-understood structure, and they both have to do with things that are *contrary to fact*.

I would get a life	if *I were* you.
You look	as if *you were* in pig heaven.
I wish	*she were* here with us.

Note that these sentences contain "wishful" information that is not true: I am not you; you are not in pig heaven, and so on. There is only one form of the verb no matter what the subject—*were*. This is called the *subjunctive*.

Sentences with the plain "if" (not "as if") clauses can go either first or last: "If I were you, I would get a life." Notice that when the "if" clause is first, it is set off by a comma.

Not Subjunctive

There are times when the "if" clause contains information that is not contrary to fact. Then we do *not* use this form.

If I was late, please excuse me. (I'm not sure whether I was late, but if I was . . .)
If he was absent, he'll make up the work later.

When "if" means "whether," we do not use the subjunctive.

The maître d' asked me if I was alone.
I felt her forehead to see if she was feverish.

Less Commonly Known Subjunctive Use

There are some expressions of *preference* or *urgency* that require the subjunctive use. These are normally ignored by many in informal speech, but they should be observed in writing to avoid the impression of ignorance or sloppiness. Be especially careful in résumés and application letters.

There is only one root form of the verb, no matter what the subject is or whether the first clause is in the present tense or the past.

Present time	**I suggest that he have more time.**
Past time	**I suggested that he have more time.**
Present time	**It's important that I be given the deed.**
Past time	**It was important that I be given the deed.**
Present time	**They ask that she write out the notes.**
Past time	**They asked that she write out the notes.**

The subjunctive is made negative by adding the word *not*.

- *I insist that you not be late.*
- *I suggest that you not go there.*

Structures with the Subjunctive

There are three basic structures used with the subjunctive:

1. Verb + *that* sentence: *I advise that he get* some treatment.

Here are the verbs in this structure:

advise	pray
arrange	prefer
ask	plead
demand	propose
desire	recommend
direct	request
insist	require
instruct	suggest
intend	urge
order	

Note: You can avoid the subjunctive by using this structure: *I advise him to get some treatment.* (This is much more common in spoken language.)

2. Noun + *that sentence: It's my advice that she receive* a third of the estate.

The nouns in this structure follow:

advice	plea
arrangement	prayer
demand	preference
desire	proposal
direction	recommendation
insistence	request
instruction	requirement
intention	suggestion
order	

3. Adjective + *that* sentence: *It's advisable that he provide* all the money.

Note: You can avoid the subjunctive by using this structure: *It's advisable for him to* . . . (This is much more common in speech.)

Here are the adjectives in this structure:

advisable	important
better	necessary
desirable	preferable
essential	right
fitting	urgent
imperative	vital

BACK AT THE RANCH

The original hardcover version of *The Horse Whisperer* was a reader's nightmare. If I hadn't paid so much for it I would have cut the infractions out one by one and sent them to the president of the publishing house. I was pleased to see that many of the problems were cleared up in the paperback version. (A houseguest left it behind; would the Grammar Lady throw good money after bad? Surely you jest.) But there remain at least twenty occasions of the nonword *alright* (it's *all right*) not to mention several subjunctive-conditional errors and a confusion between *lie* and *lay*. While these are not so interfering with the narrative, they are frequent enough to be distracting, and more than once I threw the book at the wall.

John Grisham has trouble with certain irregular past tense verbs. In the first twenty pages of *The Partner*, he uses *shrunk* instead of

---

✳**Goofy Goof:** My husband, who is in a wheelchair, received a letter from the state that began with this sentence: "The person with the disability placard listed above will soon expire." At least it's provided a few laughs.

shrank (". . . his mileage shrunk as his weight ballooned"); *sat* instead of *set* ("Guy slowly sat the mineral water on the table . . .") It is probably true that in a hundred years these verbs will be regularized, but not yet and it's silly for a major best-selling author to get them wrong.

Sometimes mistakes with irregular verbs can influence one's karma. On *Jeopardy!*, during the chat time between rounds, a contestant recounted how his alarm "had rang . . ." I immediately started rooting against him. Another, telling about losing his wedding ring while golfing said, "I had tooken off my ring." He lost. Well, don't you think he deserved it? These folks are supposed to be among our best and brightest. Just goes to show that smart doesn't mean good language use, but then most of the examples in this chapter show the same thing.

Even with all the language change that has taken place since English crossed the Atlantic, there are still more than 150 irregular verbs. Some are rather obscure (strive/strove/striven) but others are so common that people don't make mistakes (go/went/gone). Because living languages change over time, there are exceptions to current rules that must be learned as individual items. New verbs that come into English have the following pattern:

Present tense: call   I call home every week.
Past tense: called   I called home last week.
Perfect: have/had called I have called home every week
                        this year.

But there are a lot of verbs that used to have a different pattern.

Present tense: go   I go to the mall on weekends.
Past tense: went   I went to the mall last weekend.
Perfect: have/had gone I have gone to the mall every weekend
                        this year.

In some cases we can see a change taking place when there are two correct forms in competition. Eventually the newer form will take over, but for a while there is some confusion.

Present tense: light	We light candles on the dinner table.
Past tense: lighted/lit	We lighted/lit the candles last night.
Perfect: have/had lighted/lit	We have lighted/lit the candles every night.

Note: The complete list of irregular verbs is found on page 253–256.

WE'VE GOT YOUR NUMBER

One reader's pet peeve is "We've got your brake parts." The poor thing must be peeved quite often. Using "have got" for "have" is so common that it made it for a while on the Pennsylvania license plates: "You've got a friend in Pennsylvania." Oh, and remember that James Taylor song? Didn't you always wonder who that friend was?

Why has "got" become the verb of choice as in "I've got five fingers" or "The running back's got number 34." If *ve* is the abbreviation for "have" and *s* for "has," then "got" seems redundant. The word is used constantly, by radio and TV personalities I consider to be literate.

PANACHE (puh-NASH/NOSH) n. Great style, flair, flamboyance. *The character of Schindler in the movie* Schindler's List *displayed panache. Many great classical actors play roles, such as Cyrano de Bergerac, that require great panache.*

When a friend of mine called AOL on their "You've got mail" message, their reply was that "You've mail" wouldn't sound right. Indeed! What about "You have mail"? Just recently, I decided to mobilize the troops to fight this one. I put up a "have got" Question of the Week on my Web site and announced: Now, here's the deal. Everyone who uses AOL sends a message that the AOL mail message is not up to standard and suggests the correct alternative. We have to get active, folks, both off and on line.

Alas, the next day this message appeared in my E-mail: "Regarding your Question of the Week on the redundant use of 'got': I'm afraid we're going to lose this battle because the phrase 'You've got mail' will soon receive a pop culture boost from the release of a Tom Hanks/Meg Ryan movie of the same name." Apparently, Hanks's and Ryan's characters meet via America Online. But of course by now the movie's been out for a while. I wonder if I liked it? That's a little too back to the future for me.

BACK TO THE PRESENT

Well, let's move on. The confusion of "bring" and "take" annoys many of us. I have noticed more and more that news reporters and other TV personalities are very confused about the two verbs. These words can be associated with "come" and "go." If you can substitute "come," use "bring"—come to the picnic, bring a salad. If you can substitute "go," use "take"—go home and take your noisy friends with you.

In a current TV commercial for candy, the children are going to

✳**Goofy Goof:** A student was writing a paper describing a classical painting—Venus kneels next to Adonis, who was killed by a bore.

visit a friend and all shout "Let's bring him some!" It should be "Let's take him some." You could write to the candy company using this slogan and complain about the poor language use.

A football fan watching a football game over the weekend heard the announcer use a word pronounced "SEG-way." The fan couldn't find it in his dictionary. The Grammar Lady to the rescue: The spelling is *segue*, and it has two pronunciations: SAY-gway or SEG-way. It's a noun or a verb meaning to move without difficulty from one thing to another. The origin is an Italian word meaning to follow, and it was originally used to describe the way one piece of music dissolved into another. O solo mio that's amore. Or is it volare?

My audience is nothing if not eclectic. It comprises football fans and National Public Radio listeners. One of the latter asked me: "Am I the only one who shudders at 'The committee is comprised of three men and four women'? I was taught that 'comprise' means 'to include or embrace' and is best used *only* in the active voice. 'The committee comprises three men and four women.' And I think the whole comprises the parts, but the parts constitute the whole (or the whole is composed of the parts). So 'Several members comprise the panel' is wrong: Several members constitute the panel. And I have even heard 'is comprised of' on National Public Radio. Horrors!"

Horrors indeed.

GOOD AND WELL

I had the mixed pleasure of hearing one morning television personality ask his sidekick, "How are you doing?" She replied, "I'm doing good."

Shouldn't she have said, "I'm doing well"? They both are correct, but the meaning is different. "I feel good" means "cheerful, in good spirits." "I feel well" means "healthy." I do good when I contribute to charity or volunteer to answer the phones during pledge time.

Grammar Points

---

collective nouns
compose/comprise
thank you/you're welcome
bring/take
pronoun abuse
subjunctive/conditional
irregular verbs
have got
go with
lay/lie
—not?
irregardless
alright
who/m
segue

WORRISOME WORD

SUPERFLUOUS (sue-PURR-flew-us) adj. More than is sufficient or required; excessive. *Jean had talked to everyone about the problem and had examined it from every imaginable point of view; it was time to make a decision. Any more discussion would be superfluous.*

THE QUIZZICAL I

Try to sort out whether to use the subjunctive.

Example: (be) I can't remember if it _____ nice yesterday. (The answer is "was"; it's possible that it was nice, and "if" means "whether.")

(be) I wish she _____ here instead of in Bosnia. (The answer is "were"; it's not possible for her to be here.)

1. (be) "If this _____ murder, I'm going to solve it," said the detective.

2. (be) If she _____ angry about the broken vase, she didn't show it.

3. (earn) It's very important that he _____ enough money for tuition.

4. (be) His voice rang out as if he _____ Laurence Olivier performing Shakespeare.

5. (be) I don't know if she _____ late or on time.

6. (be) If the paint _____ wet, you'd get marks on your slacks.

7. (possesses) I think she _____ the intelligence and ambition to succeed.

8. (be) I wish it _____ the 1980s again.

9. (provide) It's necessary that the company _____ the information.

10. (be) If the political climate _____(neg.) such a mess, we'd all be a lot happier.

THE QUIZZICAL I

Which form of the verb do you need in this sentence? "She has run/ran her way into people's hearts." You need the past participle "run." The verb tense in this sentence is called the *Present Perfect*. It is formed by the verb "**has/have**"+the past participle. Here are some other examples:

We *have seen* the home team win every game.
He *has gone* to the mountains on vacation for ten years.
I *have written* the recipe four times and still can't find it.

With "regular" verbs, there is no problem because the past and the past participle forms are the same: "I *closed/have closed* the door." But the "irregular" verbs sometimes have different forms: "I *went (past)/have gone (present perfect) to the movies.*"

Got that? Good, here's a quiz on it. Choose the verb form to make the present perfect.

1. We have *chose/chosen* the new captain.

2. He has *seen/saw* the award-winning movie.

3. Have you *rode/ridden* in the new buses?

4. They have *came/come* late for every performance.

5. Has she *given/gave* him the present?

6. I have *began/begun* a new exercise program.

7. Have you *did/done* the crossword puzzle?

8. The new car has *broken/broke* down three times in three weeks.

9. They haven't *spoke/spoken* to her for years.

10. You've *torn/tore* the book.

Typo of the Weak

From an otherwise wholesome Midwest summer camp for kiddies. This camp's bulletin will be duly deposited in our Special After-Hours Scavenger Hunt for Counselors Only file.

A prize will be given to anybody who finds a four-leaf lover.

Typo of the Weak

From a San Francisco–area techno-firm's flack piece. It will be duly deposited in our Unfortunate Moment of Corporate Candor file.

[Engulf & Devour] has grown dramatically over the past seven years, largely through the purchase of many smaller, desperate companies.

Typo of the Weak

From a telecommunications contractor's technical paper. This, we assume, will happen only while their husbands are at sea.

These brides will support eight, sixteen, or thirty-two ports.

Chapter Four

The Life of the Party

Nothing illustrates the nature and speed of language change better than its use in social situations. My brother and I were not allowed to say "Shut up!" to each other. Words over which my mother threatened to "wash out your mouths with soap" for saying are now commonplace.

When we first moved to this neighborhood, thirty or so years ago, we found a nice, small-town mix of older folks and families with teenagers and small kids. The area reminded me of my 1950s hometown in upstate New York. Kids played basketball by the hour and waged touch-football games in the street. In this part of Pennsylvania, people—including my husband—vote Republican. When I registered as a Democrat, neighbors actually called to inquire about our "mixed marriage." (This was well ahead of Matalin and Carville.)

Over the years the town demographics have changed. There are now ten lawyers named Mike on every block, a sport utility vehicle in every driveway, and two big dogs—a black one and a brown one—in every yard. Pardon me while I yawn.

Before a recent Little League game, one of the Republican

lawyers named Mike asked his eight-year-old son, "Are you right-handed or left?" Just another example of the GOP's family values.

But I digress. Except for invitations, social interaction consists mainly of the spoken word. Fashions of speech change fairly rapidly. They change quickly because teenagers design their speech to exclude adults. As soon as we crack the teen-speak code, the teens have grown up—to be replaced by a new generation using a new language that needs to be decrypted.

Right now, "What's up?" is a popular, informal greeting. The young person in our house and her friends have shortened it even more, to " 'Sup?"

Here is an example that hit the young and hip set a few years back and disappeared almost instantly. It'll give you hope about this sort of thing. A reader mentioned that she'd seen the expression "totally tubular" a couple of times—once describing a fund-raising event and once in an ad for some kind of merchandise. She had no idea what it meant; even the people running the event didn't know. According to my teenage slang adviser, it means "awesome." It has nothing to do with tubes, and is already passé among the users of such language. Then someone reported that the term "tubular" was originally a surfing term. When conditions are exactly right the ocean waves form a tube just before they break. A very skilled surfer can maneuver through this tube for an "awesome" ride. This sounded quite plausible—a lot of recent slang has arisen from California surfing jargon. It would also explain why my East Coast teen adviser was not aware of the origin.

WORRISOME WORD

PEJORATIVE (puh/pih-JOR-uh-tiv) adj. Tending to make something seem less worthwhile or valuable than it is; belittling, derogatory. *The new kid made himself very unpopular with his pejorative remarks about the school and his new acquaintances.*

A caller recently complained that she heard her children saying "It was so fun," rather than "It was fun." I told her that this is an example of the type of nongrammatical teen-speak that drives adults crazy. Most of it passes out of the language as quickly as it enters. Did the phrase "totally tubular" ever make it into the *Oxford English Dictionary?*

When I speak to multigenerational groups, I poll the audience for the pronunciation of the word *mauve.* The boomers and Xers, to a man—actually, isn't it a woman's word?—pronounce the *au* like the *o* in "moth." Older generations pronounce the *au* as the long *o* in "both." Dictionaries still prefer the second pronunciation—apparently because boomers don't edit dictionaries.

KEEPING UP (CONVERSATIONALLY) WITH THE JONESES

My older callers frequently complain about changes in the language. These changes often involve something the linguists call phatic language—formulas of speech without literal meaning that open and close conversations, change topics, and so on.

One man called to mourn the use of the phrase "You're welcome." "You're welcome" seems to have been replaced in formal interview situations by a repeated "thank you," without the contrastive stress (thank *you*). Younger people use "no problem" or even "no problemo."

Do you think we could start a movement to save endangered language forms?

Another reader wondered whether he had been properly acknowledged for returning a lost library card to the institution's front desk.

"Miss," he said to the librarian, "I found this card."

"Umm hmmm," she said, taking it and smiling. My caller took umbrage, thinking he had been cheated on the prerequisite "Thank you." I disagree.

Once, accompanying my mother to the doctor's office, I suffered an allergic reaction to an insect bite. The doctor injected adrenaline, called 911, and asked her staff to look after my mother until I got out of the hospital a few hours later. The good physician rated flowers and a note.

There is an acceptable range of responses for a range of favors performed. Big favors get flowers. Little ones get "thank yous" or "umm hmmms." People are only entitled to get upset when there is no response at all. I do not send flowers and notes to persons who hold the door open for me, and neither should you. (Now you see why I am sometimes referred to as the Ms. Manners of Grammar.)

Another caller noticed that many news anchors, both local and national, thank reporters after airing one of their stories. My caller wondered whether Americans have started to thank colleagues too much. After all, aren't the reporters just doing their jobs? To me, though, it seems polite to say something after someone has given a report. It also signals that the segment is over—the perfect use of phatic language.

People for whom English is not their native language sometimes complain that when they say "Good morning," Americans respond with a weather report.

Mrs. Sanchez says, "Good morning, Mr. Jones."

Mr. Jones replies, "Good morning, Mrs. Sanchez. Isn't this a beautiful day?"

Mrs. Sanchez thinks that the phrase "Good morning" had nothing to do with the weather. Rather, to her it means, "I wish you a good morning." I think disagreements about language are part of the fun,

---

✳**Goofy Goof:** X resigned due to retirement.

but "Good morning" is a phrase empty of literal meaning, like "Hello." Of course, you wish some people a "good morning" and they snap, "What's good about it?"

One caller had grown very tired of people "ordering her" to "Have a nice day." "What's with all this 'Have a nice day!' stuff?" she grumbled. "I don't want people telling me what kind of day to have!" I considered suggesting that she up her Prozac dosage, but as I keep saying, my mother raised me to be polite. So I explained that greetings such as "Hello" and "How do you do?" and partings such as "It was nice to meet you" contain no meaning. Their sole purpose is to make a conversation possible, and to mark its conclusion.

Speaking of "Have a nice day," some people, mostly Californians, now substitute the phrase for "Goodbye." These Californians— mostly San Diegans—probably feel that the phrase "Have a nice day" is more sincere than a pat "Goodbye." However, the function of these partings is the same—to mark the end of the conversation. "Have a nice day" will become pat soon enough, if it hasn't already.

People understand phatic exchanges no better than they understand other language rules. A caller asked me if it is appropriate to respond "Fine, thank you," when a new acquaintance asks, "How do you do?" It is not. The appropriate response to "How do you do?" is "How do you do?" "Fine, thank you" is the response to "How are you?"—a question usually posed by a person you have previously met.

Phatic requests are often phrased in ways that give offense where none was intended. A woman reported annoyance with people who ask, "Can you spell your last name for me?" She felt like asking if she looked too dumb to spell her name. I suggested she respond with, "Yes, I can. Would you like me to?"

ANSWERING MACHINES AND OTHER TECHNOLOGICAL CHANGES

Technological changes also affect language use. People drive around with cellular phones pressed to their ears. Of course, the Grammar Lady always pulls over when her cell phone rings. Someone might ask a truly breathtaking question, such as whether to put an apostrophe after the name on holiday cards. "With love from the Smith's!?" This question never fails to leave me apoplectic.

Answering machines are a major concern. I don't have one for the Hotline. I used to. I used to return calls slavishly. My message-leaving callers rattled off their numbers so quickly that I had to listen to the whole message two or three times in order to copy it down. Long-winded types ended up using all the message tape. Then I left a window open during a rainstorm, and a couple of weeks passed before I realized the machine no longer worked. (I'm not really technologically challenged. It's just that weather reports bore me, so I never listen to them.) By that time, I'd grown used to the luxury of not returning phone calls.

But those who do use answering machines keep asking me when we're going to establish rules for leaving messages. We do need rules. A friend complained to me that a young woman left her name and the name of her company on his answering machine. The young woman then added, "My number's in the book."

It's important to make a distinction between leaving an informal message for someone you know and calling a stranger or business associate. Friends probably have your number. They probably recognize your voice, and they certainly know your last name. A stranger doesn't know anything about you. Your message is your first impression. If you want to receive a return call, the message should be polite, clear, and brief. Speak slowly enough so that the recipient can jot down the pertinent information without having to replay the message.

A format such as the following might work. Leave your

- Name. If you have an unusual last name, spell it.
- Message.
- Number. Say it once, then repeat it.

Your script might read: "Hello. This is June Deere. I'm calling about the position you advertised. My telephone number is 555 (pause) 1212. That's 555-1212." (And say "one, two, one, two," not "twelve-twelve.")

Sometimes, intonation causes problems in telephone discussions. My callers say they notice that young people often use a rising intonation at the end of every sentence, as if every statement were a question. I have noticed this trend, too. It unnerves me. Young people speaking on the telephone often introduce themselves with a rising note at the end. "Hi. This is Jane Doooeeee?" I'm tempted to ask, "Are you sure?"

MINDING OTHER PEOPLE'S MANNERS

Using incorrect language can have major consequences, changing a person's life, especially a social life. Remember my daughter's rejection of her inarticulate suitor, for instance?

Correcting someone's language, especially pronunciation, is taboo in our culture. My mother once clucked at me when I corrected one of my English as a second language students at a party. Today, as the incorrect use of language continues to run rampant, some people feel a responsibility to help their friends with this "issue."

A woman called about her friend, a former union leader who had been appointed to a highly visible position with a public fund-raising organization. He had asked her for help with his language. He seemed to know his grammar and pronunciation needed some improvement. My caller was frustrated, though, because her friend didn't seem to accept the changes she suggested. I told her that changing one's language use is very difficult for an adult. A dramatic change in your speech can be viewed as rejection by the people who knew you when you spoke in a more "down-to-earth" manner. I suggested my caller urge her friend to consider that there are different ways of speaking—the sociolinguistics I discussed in the second chapter. Perhaps he could grow to understand that, in his new position, the expectations were different. She didn't call back, so I don't know what happened.

I heard about another technique that might be helpful with adults. It's called mimicking—whenever the goofer says something wrong, take the next available occasion to say the exact same thing yourself. In the exchange I overheard, the offending partner was so shocked to hear this language from the usually correct spouse that change began right away.

A grandmother was so put off by her grandson's "likes" and "ya knows" that she started counting aloud every time one came up. The kid finally threw up his hands and said, "I can't say a thing." She reported that he had begun to clean up his speech act, but she didn't let up on the counting until it was completely "like"-free.

A woman for whom English is not her native language called to ask why the word *say* is pronounced with a long *a* sound, but the word *says* isn't. She was aggrieved because her friends kept correcting her to say "sez." I told her that many irregular verbs have a different pronunciation for the part that goes with "it/he/she." (I do/she does, I have/he has, I am/it is.) In older versions of English, each verb agreed with its subject, but most of the endings have been lost over time. This remnant is a concerted attempt to make life miserable. Just be glad most of you don't have to learn English as a foreign language.

One caller has a friend who ends many sentences with "and etc." Since "etc." means "and so on," her use of "and etc." seems redundant. The frequency of this expression in her speech is irritating enough, but her misuse of it drives friends to distraction. Similarly, another friend frequently says "and so on and so forth." Wouldn't one or the other be correct ("and so on" or "and so forth")?

My caller suggested I place a hint in my column, warning readers of the perils of redundant speech. I placed the hint. Now what effect do you think this chapter will have on your friends? Buy a copy of the book for your linguistically challenged buddies and highlight pertinent passages. This is just a suggestion from my tender and concerned publishers.

Another caller related that she once had occasion to tell a story about a petty theft at the horseback-riding school her daughter attends. At the end of the story, one listener asked: "Are they going to persecute them?" My caller responded that she didn't know about persecution, but the owners were mad enough to prosecute. I think that this qualifies for listing in our Gentle Correction section.

The Grammar Lady's Internet site had a long message board discussion on the topic of the Gentle Correction of those who misuse the English language. I thought you'd find the exchange both helpful and entertaining, so I took the liberty of providing you with the following excerpt:

YE OLDE GRAMMARIAN: How might I politely, gently, yet effectively explain to a friend that her pronunciation of "ebullient" is incorrect? (She says EBB-you-lent, not eh-BULL-yent.) How do I correct her when she says "paroxm" (puh-ROCKS-em) instead of "paroxysm" (puh-ROCK-sihz-em)? And how can I get her to understand the correct use of the word *myriad*? I've tried repeating the former two words correctly soon after she mispronounces them: that does not work. I've tried using "myriad" in myriad sentences, to no avail. (And, frankly, I'm beginning to feel that my overuse of the word is perceived as an affectation.) Any suggestions?

JOHN BOY: You might refresh her memory with the story of the Emperor's New Clothes. Put a child's copy of it on her desk/chair. During my youth, my time of raging hormones, I tried to snow a fair damsel with my use of the word *poignant.* Only I pronounced the *g* as it is pronounced in "pregnant." She politely corrected my pronunciation. I kissed her good night, and slid under and out the door. She didn't even have to open it. We didn't pan out, but I very, very fortunately ended up marrying her roommate—who has yet to hear me mispronounce "poyniant." How do we learn if we're not taught?

KD: If you are a lot older than she is, you could take the avuncular "This is for your own good" approach and tell her directly. Or you could pretend you didn't understand. You could say, "What was that? Oh, you mean . . ." then fill in the correct word.

LD: Several years ago I used the word *paradigm,* pronouncing it "paradijim." I was immediately corrected by a man my junior of some twenty-five years. He asked, "You mean 'paradime?'" "Of course, I do," I replied, as I dropped a dictionary on my foot.

INDIOLEE: What if you told the lady that you admired her

intelligence and that, as a grammarian, you hated to think that others' perceptions of her might be affected by her mispronunciations? Ask her whether she would like you to tell her about any words she mispronounces. I think she'll give you instant permission.

When yours truly was trotting around New York City to bring the very pages you are now reading to fruition, the publishers and editors I met with considered how to point out someone's error diplomatically a fascinating question. One editor had a brilliant solution, presuming the speakers are not from the same place, or of the same age group. He suggested saying, "Is that the way they say it in your town nowadays? When I was growing up in Boston, we pronounced it 'myriad.' Let's check the dictionary."

One of my favorite examples of Gentle Correction in a social setting involves a well-spoken woman who invited a friend for tea. The friend did not like the dog sniffing around the tea cakes, so she said "Lay down." Nothing happened. Thinking the dog to be deaf as well as ill-trained, she tried again, more forcefully, "Lay down!" Entering the room, the hostess saw what was happening and said, "Lie down." The dog instantly lay down.

INVITATIONS AND ANNOUNCEMENTS

Before I get into the specific mechanics of invitations, I must let my general feelings on the subject be known. I know I am going against modern practice here when I say how much I *hate* cutesy-poo wording on wedding invitations. Everyone knows that a wedding is the beginning of a couple's new life together, so why can't couples (and I know this is a radical concept) just *invite people to a wedding*? What's wrong with a simple

> Jennifer Whatever and Joseph Whatnot request the honor of your presence at their wedding, which will be June X at some o'clock at Our Lady of Propriety Church

The Grammar Lady beseeches you, don't try to be clever, and for goodness sake, don't try to be original, because you probably won't succeed, and if you do, you will probably just confuse or offend people. If you want them at your wedding, just ask them to come. Now then, I am ready to answer a few genuine questions about down-to-earth invitations.

Many people have a terrible time with the word *you*. On invitations, it's hard to make it plain who is included. This is a widespread problem. The word *you* can include only the person spoken to, any part of, or all of the people addressed. Many other languages have separate words for the singular you (tu/du) and the plural you (vous/usted/Sie). Older forms of English had a singular form, "thou," as in "Thou shalt not kill." Obviously that's fallen out of use. I mean the word *thou*, not the idea that it's better not to kill. Standard English doesn't have a form of "you" that specifies a plural. (This is the reason that regional dialects invent plural forms. In the South it's y'all; in Canada and Brooklyn it's youse; in Pittsburgh it's yunz.) So write your invitations as specifically as possible: "I'd like you" or "I'd like you and Jack" or "I'd like you and Jack and the kids . . ."

WORRISOME WORD

OBDURATE (ahb-DUHR/DyUHR-it) adj. Obstinate, inflexible, unbending. *The visitor was obdurate about keeping to his home schedule, which made life difficult for the California family who had very different lives.*

A wedding program I perused listed the attendants' first and last names with no titles except for two, which were listed as Dr. So-and-So. Academic and professional titles are used in the business/work world to establish rank and position. Unless the wedding is a royal or diplomatic function, the use of these titles is inappropriate.

Another wedding invitation query involved the use of Ms. or Miss to address an older single woman. Ms. is a term of address in the business world where the marital status of a woman is irrelevant. In a social setting, Miss and Mrs. are the appropriate titles.

Then there was the bride who wanted to invite a couple made up of a man and a very independent woman. The inviter wanted to recognize her independence and address it to "Mr. and Mrs. Frank and Sandra Jones." Let's set aside the fact that she is not "Mrs. Sandra Jones." If the couple has the same last name, the only correct way to address a social invitation to them is "Mr. and Mrs. Frank Jones." A wedding invitation is not the place to be making a political statement.

A family was preparing an engagement announcement for their daughter to appear in our local newspaper. The form the paper provided had the following line: "The bride-elect graduated from _____." They wanted to know if it should be "bride-elect" or "bride-to-be" and "graduated from" or "was graduated from"? I, too, prefer "bride-to-be." I agree that "was graduated from" is correct; however, in an engagement, I think "the bride-to-be is a graduate of X University" flows more smoothly. I laughed about "bride-elect" all day—as if she beat the other candidates.

Proud new parents of twins asked, "Should the birth announcement read 'Our family has doubled' or 'Our family have doubled?' I told them that family is a collective noun that can be either singular

---

❋**Goofy Goof:** From a student paper: Five years ago at the age of twelve my grandmother died.

or plural depending on the context. I certainly hope they want to think of "family" as a single unit, so it should read "has doubled."

THE ART OF GIVING

Some readers were hosting a fiftieth anniversary party for their parents. The feted couple neither needed, nor had room for, a plethora of presents. Their offspring wanted to know how to discourage guests from bringing gifts. Miss Manners says it is impolite to say "No gifts" on an invitation. (One should not be thinking of gifts when giving a party, apparently.) I suggested that the kids inform their guests that they were compiling a photo album for their parents. They could ask each guest to contribute a few photos, clearly labeled. That way, the celebrating couple has a meaningful memento of the occasion, and their house does not become cluttered with unneeded (and, frankly, unwanted) gifts.

A divorced woman and her grown son were sending a joint wedding gift to some friends. They wondered how to sign the card. I suggested they sign their names, "Edie Jones and (her) son, Rick."

THE ART OF THANKING

Someone writing a thank-you note wondered whether she should express appreciation for *a* unique gift or *an* unique gift. Even though the word begins with the vowel *u*, it has the sound of the consonant *y* (a yellow flower). Use the word *a*. The same rule applies in "a one-year subscription" because the *o* sounds like a *w*.

The proper use of the phrase "thank you" itself has caused some confusion of late. An early morning Hotline call left the Grammar Lady glum for about an hour. It ran something like this.

CALLER: When does "thank you" have an apostrophe?
ME: I can't really think of any time it would.
CALLER: When it's possessive!
ME: When could "thank you" possibly be possessive?
CALLER: Lots of times!

After she hung up I thought perhaps I could buy a Beanie Baby, and name it "Thank You." Then I could see using the possessive form. "Look at Thank You's new wardrobe!" Really, dear, that is the only possessive use of "thank you" that I can imagine.

WHAT'S IN A NAME?

When our daughter was small she called all adults without a family title (Grandma, Aunt, Uncle, and so on) by Mr./Mrs./Miss plus their last name. Some of the lawyers-named-Mike crowd allow their children, up to the age of five, to call all nonrelated adults by their first names. When the poor kids reach age six, they have to follow the Mr./Mrs. rule. I never had lengthy conversations with these folks to find out the source of this rule because no child who called me by my first name was ever invited back to my home.

The lawyers-named-Mike invaded my town in the 1970s and 1980s. Some had moved here from other parts of the country. It was not easy to talk to these newcomers because their outlook seemed so different from our homegrown philosophies. All of a sudden, in the late 1970s, a neighborly community of shared ladders, power tools, and recipes had turned into a competitive, me-first arena that revered buying services and precluded "doing it yourself" and sharing.

I wonder if the myriad questions I receive on correct forms of address began to develop at about this time. I've divided them into convenient groups for your perusal. You can scan the subheadings for the category you most urgently need, although I do hope you won't need this first one too often.

Widows

Some ladies have very strong opinions on the subject of how to address a widow. One said she was a widow and liked to be addressed as "Mrs. Frances S." She also liked the use of her husband's name: "Mrs. Bruce S." Another found it odd that women seem to have a problem with how they are addressed, whether widowed or not. She changed her maiden name to match her husband's when they were married; however, she did not lose her *identity* when she married him. She had never used "Mrs. Michael D. S.," as her name, "Janet L.," was given to her when she was born. If she is to be addressed by her married name, she prefers "Mrs. Janet L. S."

And some readers have questions:

One wondered how a woman is addressed when her husband has died. Does "Mrs. John Smith" become "Mrs. Mary Smith"? Certainly not. She remains "Mrs. John Smith" until she remarries. Divorced women who keep the ex-husband's surname often use Mrs. with their first name—especially if they have young children.

Someone even had the temerity to ask if this topic wasn't an etiquette question rather than a grammar question. She thought most modern widows preferred to be addressed by their given names, such as "Mrs. Mary Smith" or "Ms. Mary Smith." On one hand this is an etiquette question, but it also involves language use and thus falls into my area of interest. Women of my grandmother's, my mother's, and my generation have used our husbands' names for social purposes, and widowhood has not changed that usage. Whether this has changed recently with "modern" widows, I don't know.

Same Sex, Same Last Name

The plural for Mr. is Messrs. It can be used if the men have the same last name or different ones: "Messrs. John and William Doe"; "Messrs. Hardy and Jones." The plural of Ms. is Mss. or Mses. I prefer Mses. because Mss. looks like the abbreviation for manuscripts. Correct usage: "Mses. Mary and Jane Doe"; "Mses. Doe and Jones."

Names Ending with *S*

A disapproving aunt was asked to help a niece who had married into a family named Mordagris. (It was not clear whether the aunt disapproved of the name or the husband.) The niece needed help with her new name with respect to the appropriate plural and possessive forms. Let's see. The plural is straightforward: add "es." "Did you invite the Mordagrises?" The plural possessive is not a problem either: add an apostrophe to the plural. "Did you enjoy the Mordagrises' party?" In the singular, there are two choices: add only the apostrophe or " 's." "I saw Judy Mordagris'" "Mordagris's husband."

WORRISOME WORD

NEFARIOUS (nih-FARE-ee-us) adj. Terribly wicked, villainous. *The teenager saw the grounding during the week after passing the driver's test as a nefarious plot; the parents saw it as a reminder to be responsible.*

Terms of Endearment

Want to send a letter to a former governor who no longer holds a political office? According to my sources, former government officials retain the titles they held in office. Seems strange.

When you address a card to two young girls, should you use "The Misses Jane and Judy Doe?" Misses is right, but drop the "The."

In a letter to a fifteen-year-old male, would you use Master? According to an etiquette manual on my shelf, the title Master is reserved for males under ten years old; so I guess "Mr." is in order.

Men Assuming Titles

If John Doe Sr. dies, John Doe Jr. becomes Sr. if there is another male of the same name after him in the line. Otherwise he becomes simply John Doe.

This change isn't always a fortunate thing from some points of view. A caller had a friend who is a "III." His grandfather was a brilliant essayist and his father an extremely successful businessman. The friend is a ne'er-do-well. If, when his grandfather and his father died, the friend stepped up from III to Jr. to Sr., he would assume their identities and credit he didn't deserve. The caller maintained that Sr., etc., should be a permanent part of the names so that history might easily identify who they were. Genealogists would heartily agree with his assessment, for more pragmatic research reasons.

Women Changing Their Names

When a woman marries and changes her surname, does she then use her maiden name as her new middle name? Does Mary Jane Jones become Mary Jane Smith or is it Mary Jones Smith? The older etiquette guide that I used to answer this question is quite clear on this issue: The woman's maiden name becomes part of the married name. However, the newer one seems to imply that either way is correct. Perhaps the fashion is changing, or perhaps it's a regional variation or matter of personal preference.

Women who are recently divorced have a lot of difficulties, the least of which I think would be use of name. One woman had taken back her maiden name, but people still called her Mrs. She didn't feel like a "Mrs." and wanted people to call her "Miss" or "Ms." I suggested she say to them, "Please call me Ms. or Miss." Or she could have a new plaque with the preferred name made for her desk. It's hard to get used to calling someone by a new name, but as time goes by it's easier.

GREETINGS AND SIGNS

People often want to know whether, when posting "Season's Greetings" on print material, the apostrophe in "Season's" is correct. If you are celebrating only one season, then using the apostrophe before *s* is certainly correct. These days, most people send greetings for Hanukkah, Christmas, Kwanzaa, and the New Year, hence the correct phrase would be "Seasons' Greetings." Don't forget to send me a card next year.

Here is the last word in this chapter. Maybe it will be the last word of every chapter. Heaven knows I have enough examples for every topic. There were a lot of arguments at a local craft shop on the subject of the "welcome" plaques that some families hang on their doors. If the family names are Lewis and Rustler, should the

---

※ **Goofy Goof:** On the cover of a rather prestigious magazine was this headline: Who do the doctors trust?

sign say "Welcome—The Rustlers" or "The Rustler's," "The Lewises" or "The Lewis's?" The words of welcome are from the people, and only an *s* or *es* is required to make the name plural (Rustlers/Lewises). If it's "Welcome to the Rustlers' House," then it's possessive. The apostrophe is added after the name is made plural: Rustlers' House, Lewises' House. Got it?

Grammar Points

---

change in social language
pronunciation of mauve
phatic language
"you're welcome"
range of "thank you" occasions
answering machine rules
titles + last names
addressing widows
addressing men with the same last name
names ending in *s*
addressing former elected officials
addressing young girls
addressing young men
mens' last names and number
women changing names
correcting others' language
wedding invitations
plural "you"
seasons' Greetings
apostrophe in name signs

Typo of the Weak

From a Charlotte, North Carolina, firm's sales manager's E-mail to the salesperson of the month (opposite sex, of course); it brings new meaning to the term "tabling the discussion."

> I understand that you doubled your [sales] quota this month. Let's meet in the conference room at 2:30. You can give me a complete rubdown.

Typo of the Weak

From a Washington, D.C., area prestigious law firm's E-mail alert; it reminds us that advanced technology is no match for throat cultures.

> We are currently experiencing problems with our voice massaging system.

Chapter *Five*

Work It Out

Many of the calls to the Grammar Hotline come from office workers who are committed to getting their correspondence and memos right. I'm almost always eager to help these folks keep their grammatically correct faces up to snuff. Most business callers keep to the spirit of the Hotline—a quick call to get it right. But then there are the hotline abusers.

A couple of years after the Hotline began, an older woman in an office in Pittsburgh started calling at least once a week with paragraph-length sentences that needed to be completely rewritten in order to make any sense of them. She had a high, annoyingly nasal voice that I recognized the first syllable into her question. Since I was new to the service and my mother had brought me up to be polite, I suffered this onslaught for weeks. Finally I could bear it no longer. Whenever she called, I immediately tuned out until I heard the final downward intonation signaling the end of the sentence, then replied, "Sounds good to me," and hung up before she could go on. She finally stopped calling, but I continued to wonder whom she found to edit her stuff.

One young woman, employed (she said) by a huge insurance

company in Philadelphia, turned to the Grammar Hotline because of her comma "issues." (People don't have *problems* these days; they have *issues*.) During her first call, she asked a question and then corrected herself, "No, that don't need a comma." Over the next two weeks, she called at least twice a day, sometimes three times, asking about commas, how to spell "validity," which she couldn't pronounce, and which I had to spell three times. On her third call of the day, I asked if she didn't have any reference books in her office and remarked, rather curtly, that I was not her private secretary. (Sorry, Mom.)

What I have learned is that there are people who shouldn't have well-paying jobs if they can't do them, and that it is not in my purview to keep them employed. The question is how they got jobs in the first place and how they are able to retain them.

It probably is a good thing that spell- and grammar checkers are so notoriously deficient. Here's a little poem that a reader sent along:

I have a spelling checker,
It came with my PC.
It clearly marks for my revue,
Mistakes I cannot sea.
I've run this poem threw it,
I'm sure your please too no

WORRISOME WORD

TACITURN (TAH—like tap—sih-turn) adj. Not inclined to talk, showing marked restraint in speaking. *Taciturn people are not good candidates for talk show hosts.* A related word is *tacit,* unspoken. *When Dad didn't say no to taking the car, we took it as a tacit agreement that we could.*

It's letter perfect in its weigh,
My spell-check tolled me sew.

One of the Recreational Grammarians who frequent my Web site remarked that a native speaker of English who needs a grammar checker for writing is in the wrong line of work. People call and ask what the passive voice is because their grammar checker said it was a bad thing.

I just ran the Word 5.1 grammar checker on the beginning paragraphs of this chapter. It reported "This verb group may be in the passive voice." *May be*? The thing doesn't have the courage of its convictions. It told me that "She asked a question" is redundant, and so it is, but in the context above, what else should I use? As to "whom she found," the advice was "Consider **who** instead of **whom**," clearly wrong. For the phrase "who needs a grammar checker" the program suggested "**checkers** instead of **checker**," another incorrect suggestion. As for the poem, all it had to say was "This appears to be a run-on sentence" and "This does not seem to be a complete sentence." What is the poor grammar-deprived office worker without a fifty-year-old secretary to do?

At times though, even humans can be recalcitrant. One office worker couldn't get a pool secretary to type the word *trough* in a letter; tough, through, and though, but not trough, even after he wrote *T-R-O-U-G-H*, because it wasn't in her dictionary. Little wonder that this set of words is often used as ammunition by spelling reformers to demonstrate the absurdity of English spelling. The secretary was probably a city dweller who wasn't familiar with a trough (rhymes with cough, a feeding or watering box for animals). The word used to be common in politics—"feeding at the public trough"—but I haven't seen it in a long time. The boss finally retrieved his letter, typed it himself, and sent it off. But he got it back because in the meantime the company had gone out of business. Spelling matters!

LOOK IT UP

The slim volume of *Strunk & White* is no longer an adequate reference for the current generation of office workers. A much more voluminous work is required (this one, O'Conner, Tarshis, Kilpatrick), but whether the recipient of such a tome would know how to use it is open to question.

Dictionaries range broadly in purpose, size, and price, and are a very personal decision. The best advice is to make note of the things you look up in a dictionary over a few weeks' time, and then go to a comprehensive bookstore to make the choice. Here are a few things to look for in making your selection.

Size. Big, complete (unabridged) dictionaries are expensive and take a lot of room in your office or home. They are also difficult for children to use because they are bulky, and it takes longer to look something up because new readers' alphabetizing skills are incomplete. An unabridged dictionary on the coffee table might impress your friends; but unless you use a dictionary every day, it probably is not a good buy. Perhaps you should look at smaller "college" dictionaries.

Pronunciation guide. Many people use a dictionary to help them pronounce new words. (One caller to the Grammar Hotline saw an "etagere" advertised for sale, knew what it was and wanted one, but didn't want to call the seller without knowing how to pronounce the word.) The guide should be complete but not contain a lot of unfamiliar symbols that require continual cross-checking—

❀**Goofy Goof:** If the hurricane hits Florida, many people's homes could be destoried.

especially with the vowels. The English vowel system is complex because we use one letter to spell many different sounds. For example, the letter *a* has three different sounds in the words *at, age,* and *art.* The job for the dictionary makers is to find three common symbols to represent the different pronunciations.

Examples.   Sample sentences showing common uses of words are very helpful, both in clarifying the meaning and helping the reader remember the word. The words in the sentences should not be any more difficult than the target word, however, or the reader is sent off on a frustrating chase through the dictionary. In the words of technology, "A good dictionary should be user-friendly."

Usage notes.   Many dictionaries comment on the usage of words in different types of situations. Many of the old dictionaries contained only the standard accepted usages. "Ain't" was not to be found and teachers could correct their charges by saying, "Ain't isn't in the dictionary." Imagine the teachers' dismay when dictionaries started including such forms! The dictionaries do comment on the usage—nonstandard, colloquial, regionalism are some of the terms used to let readers make their own decisions about whether they want to use the term.

One final comment—forms of speech change much more rapidly than written forms of language, and many spoken items never make it to the written language (slang, for example). For this reason, you will need to buy several dictionaries during your reading life. Find

WORRISOME WORD

OBSTREPEROUS (uhb-STREP-er-us) adj. Out of control in a noisy way; boisterous, clamorous. *The parents made no effort to control their obstreperous children as they stood on the chairs in the waiting room and shouted at each other.*

one that you like and consider its new editions when it's time for a new one.

REPORT LINGO

The business community seems to run on meetings and reports; and if the questions I receive regarding reports are any indication, this country is in big trouble. I can't understand why the Dow hasn't disappeared by now. Speaking of numbers, I get a lot of mail about how to use them in reports. Why, I've known coworkers who have practically come to fisticuffs over beginning a sentence with a number—"1988 was a very good year for Château Haute Bas," for example. Toni Morrison did it at the beginning of *Beloved* and it took me several pages to get over it. While Nobel Prize winners are allowed some poetic license, it is generally not a good idea to begin with numerals because it is difficult for the reader to understand what the number means without a context. We don't know whether it is "nineteen eighty-eight" or "one thousand nine hundred eighty-eight" until we get to the word *year*, and if we've made the wrong guess, we have to reread to get the correct meaning.

There are pages and pages of rules detailing numbers (a spelled-out number, e.g., ten) versus numerals (the actual symbol for the number, e.g., 10), and they're nicely covered in the journalism and publishing style manuals. For general writing, here are The Grammar Lady's helpful hints. So much more digestible, aren't they?

1. Don't begin a sentence with a numeral.
2. Use figures if the number has more than two words. Examples: 1,560,240; $596.40; 1895. But: two dollars; fifty-five years old.

3. Be kind to the reader. Inconsistent usage of words and figures is very difficult to read. If there is no other rule to guide the writing, this should be the overriding one: look at the page for readability. Scientific writing is a different game, so follow the rules of your field.

From numbers, we can move gracefully into percentages. With words like *percent*, the noun that follows determines the verb:

- Eighty percent of the income goes for food.
- Eighty percent of the workers live near the plant.

Quick, what should the verb be in the following sentence? "More than 85 percent of the workforce is/are women." You need to decide whether the collective *workforce* is singular or plural. Or you could hedge your bets and add "is made up of women." When it comes to grammar, I always say, "When in doubt, rewrite."

People often take exception to my pronouncement that the noun after *85 percent of* determines whether the verb is singular or plural. It seems many people have committed to memory the rule "the object of a preposition is never the subject of the sentence." Since *of* is a preposition, the reasoning goes, the noun after it cannot be the subject. However, there are a couple of notable exceptions (aren't there always?) including *percent* and *majority*. The major exception concerns the SAMAN words, as one reader named them: *some, all, most, any,* and *none*. These words refer directly to the noun that follows and it determines the number of the verb. Consider:

Some of the paper is blue. Some of the papers are wet.
Most of the book was thrilling. Most of the books were thrilling.
Ten percent of the voters are not voting.
Ten percent of the investment is in cash.

Where the "object of the preposition" rule works is when there are two concrete nouns:

That group of children is making too much noise.
The safety and health of the boy were the most important concerns.

People can be *very* stubborn on this same topic. One quibbler really thought she had me with this argument: "The subject—think about what the word means—of a sentence is what it talks about. The word *water* in the following sentence is *not* the subject: Some of the water in the lake has evaporated. Why? The verb *has* agrees with *some*, the subject. Only some has evaporated, not all of it, and that's what the sentence talks about, the part that has evaporated. Granted, the object of the preposition determines the number of the subject, but water is clearly *not* the subject. *Some* is." Now I will grant you that *some* is the grammatical subject but the verb is governed by the word after the preposition. If I asked you "What has evaporated?" and you answered, "Some," we wouldn't have had a very successful communication, now would we?

MAKE MINE MS.

A lot of business questions have to do with how to address people in written correspondence. In a business letter to a corporation, for example, would it be permissible to use "Gentleperson" as the salutation? Not if you are writing to my corporation. The pursuit of politically correct language has reached absurd lows. First, "chairman," which is neutral in regard to gender, was replaced by "chairperson" (consider human/huperson! or woman/woperson!) and then by a piece of furniture—"chair." Let's all sit down on that chair and get a grip.

What salutation should be used when responding to a business office inquiry if no name is provided? Now honestly, why would someone ask a question and not provide a name for a response? In any case, I like "Dear Correspondent" for a simple, down-to-earth salutation solution. The opposite situation occurs when people seem quite taken with other people's fancy titles and want to toss them in anywhere they can. I'm always being asked questions such as "How should I address a letter to a businessman who holds a Ph.D.?" As a rule, business people don't use academic or other honorary titles. Mr. John Doe, not Dr. John Doe, is almost always proper.

Esquire is another title I need to explain frequently. What does "Esq." mean and how is it used? Esq. is the abbreviation for Esquire, which is used following the surnames of people in the American bar (that's the law, not mixed drinks). It is used on the envelope and inside address of a letter, but not in the salutation or with any other titles (Ms., Dr., The Honorable) accompanying the name. The letter might start off this way:

Jane R. Doe, Esq.
Attorney-at-Law

Dear Ms. Doe,

After I spent a whole column on the use of Ms. versus Miss in addressing a single woman, I thought I had exhausted the subject. Wouldn't you know a reader came up with yet another variation on the theme, saying, "As someone who is interested in correct grammar, punctuation, and feminism, I question why you used a period after Ms? Ms is not an abbreviation." Well, I'm not quite sure what the period (or not) after Ms. has to do with feminism. However, since the title was intended for use in the business world, I use business-related publications as guides to accepted usage. Two. up-to-date secretaries' manuals and the unabridged dictionary have Ms. with a period. Perhaps the editors thought Ms. *was* an abbreviation, or perhaps they were *Mstaken.*

The whole Ms. controversy met up with Esquire early in Clinton's first administration when I suggested addressing Hillary as Mrs. William Clinton. After hordes of calls and letters I threw in the towel: Okay! Okay! (Ms.) Hillary R. (Rodham) Clinton, (Esq.) Just don't use both Ms. and Esq. together.

One footnote on the subject of business letters: The postal service is trying to do away with all punctuation in addresses on envelopes, but that doesn't make it correct in the text of a letter, at least not according to my secretarial reference manual. The postal service recommends the address be in all capital letters with a comma between the city and state as the only punctuation. The address on the inside of the letter should be in traditional form. One of life's little hassles is that this requires typing the address twice. But I think we can all handle that, can't we?

THIS AND THAT

Since there is no longer a carbon copy of a letter—how many of you ever saw a carbon copy? Remember all that terrible ink rubbing off on your hands and ruining your clothes?—what do we put at the bottom of a letter when we send a copy to someone? The most wonderful solution is to continue to use cc, but, if anyone asks, call it a "courtesy copy." Clever, isn't it?

✳Goofy Goof: Here is a quote by a national network anchor who should know better: "Those of we who . . ."

Here's an apostrophe question that popped up on my Web site: Should *minds* be possessive in the phrase "your performance in the minds' of the employers"? The question reminds me of my New Year's resolution regarding restoration of the apostrophe to proper usage. A reader, Virginia Peden, sent along this poem that she wrote on the subject.

> The poor little apostrophe
> Is so put upon;
> It's often where it shouldn't be
> And where it should, it's gone.

At any rate, it's the employers who possess the minds. *Minds* is merely plural. Bet you knew that.

WE'RE ALL CONNECTED—AND HOW

Business telephone call protocol is crucial. When company representatives answer calls, they have no way of knowing whether it's a curmudgeon like me on the other end or a clueless kid. Trust me, polite and correct are the order of the day. We have been known to move our bank accounts and our credit cards away from companies whose "representatives" don't get it right.

Identifying oneself in telephone calls as "This is her" is one such offense. As it's often followed by "Where you at?" you can see why our nerves are ragged after repeated attempts at tactful correction. Sometimes, tactful correction is not enough. That's when you need to pull out the big grammar guns: Send a supply of grammar goof stickers, or compile a list of office pet peeves with checkoff boxes.

In any case, one should identify oneself with "This is she/he," but many people think this is too formal. Other acceptable forms are "Speaking," and "This is (name)." "Where you at?" probably requires the attention of the office manager because it could reflect badly on a caller's perception of the company as a professional group.

One woman lamented that she and her husband both work at home on different businesses. When she is the only one there, she answers his phone for him. I must say, I am touched by such matrimonial devotion. I wonder if I could get Charlie to answer the Hotline while I go on that Caribbean cruise I've been plotting? Anyway, often the female secretaries of his customers, upon hearing her voice, assume she is his secretary and speak very rudely. Later when her husband returns the calls, the secretaries are all sweetness and light. This is not only very annoying but puts the wife in a bad mood. Her marriage is in jeopardy! Actually, I think it's the working at home together that's the problem. See pages 17–18 for more on this subject. Short of screening the calls with an answering machine, the only approach I can think of is a direct yet ever so polite challenge: "Excuse me, why are you using that tone of voice?" or "Is there some particular reason you feel you can talk to me that way?" Why anyone would be rude on the phone under any circumstances is a mystery, right up there on a par with how babies are born, as far as I'm concerned.

WORRISOME WORD

INSOUCIANT (in-SUE-see-uhnt) adj. Free from anxiety, concern, or worry; carefree; nonchalant. *The fable of the insouciant grasshopper and the workaholic ant illustrates basic personality differences.*

BUSINESS E-MAIL

With the advent of personal computers, writing has been making a comeback of sorts in the guise of E-mail. People who haven't put pen to paper in years now feel empowered to send reams of messages to you-know-whom requesting help with all nature of things to do with language and grammar. I do not mind typos because E-mail is a hurry-up medium; but when there are no capital letters or punctuation in an E-mail query, I don't respond. Those messages are hard to read, and I don't have time to decipher them. If people want my advice about language use, they need to show they are going to use it to good advantage. I also have great sympathy for people for whom English is not their native language and young students. But I have great trouble with people who don't know or can't say what they want to know. Here are some recent E-mail messages. I am reproducing them here verbatim.

This person asked just the right sort of question at first, but then slipped into "whine-gimme" mode reminiscent of the secretaries at the beginning of this chapter.

> Hi,
>   I'm working on a marketing slipsheet.
> 1) In the title "Working Toward Your Goals in Public Health," should the word be *towards* or *toward*.
> 2) Do you have any suggestions for writing paragraphs? I understand you start with a introductory sentence then build on it. However, I really struggle when writing. Any tips would be appreciated. Especially ones related to flow and organization.
>   Thank you.

I answered:

1) Toward. 2) There are zillions of books out there telling folks how to write. Find one that addresses your concerns and buy it.

She was offended that I wouldn't help her and accused me of not knowing the answer.

This guy didn't even bother with a salutation:

Please describe the proper use of the semicolon
This will settle an argument
Thanks

Is individual effort totally dead? Suppose I gave out the wrong information and he loses the bet. Doesn't he want to be sure he's right? I don't get it. So I answered:

Go to your local bookstore. In the reference section you will find many interesting books on grammar and punctuation.

Here's an example of what I *really* object to: a voluminous E-mail with no real point and numerous questions without possibility of coherent answer.

Dear Grammar Lady,

I was attempting to relate some information concerning the difference between "might" and "may" to a friend, but in the process, I encountered a bit of difficulty with punctuation. Specifically, the problem concerns question marks and quotation marks. I know that a question mark goes inside quotation marks, but in this case there is a quote within a quote. Which (if any) of the two sentences below is punctuated correctly?

a) Imagine your boss asks, "Which would you rather hear: 'You may get a raise,' or 'You might get a raise'?"
b) Imagine your boss asks, "Which would you rather hear: 'You may get a raise,' or 'You might get a raise?'"

To make matters worse, I initially attempted to phrase the sentence in the following manner. (I will use three asterisks to represent the series of punctuation marks in question.)

If your boss asks you, "Which would you rather hear: 'You may get a raise,' or 'You might get a raise' you should select the statement using "may."

In this case, how would the space indicated by the three asterisks be punctuated? I assume that a comma would be needed to separate the clause that begins "you should," but where it should be placed in relation to the other punctuation marks is a mystery to me.

I admit that, for the most part, I am writing out of curiosity, but I sincerely appreciate any help you may be able to provide me.

That there were no asterisks made me impatient so I told him to stop losing sleep over this kind of thing. He replied a week later and complained that I hadn't answered his question.

What are we to make of this stuff? On the one hand I'm really glad people are writing and seem concerned for the most part about getting it right. The rules of E-mail should be the same as for any other kind of writing.

WORRISOME WORD

VERDANT (VUR—rhymes with fur—dent) adj. Green with growing plants. *I love the verdant vistas of the Northeast in the spring—until it's time to cut the grass.*

1. Figure out what you want to say. (If you don't know, don't send it.)
2. Read it over before you send it so that #1 is met.
3. Be concise, but give enough information so that the recipient knows what you need. (People who read a lot of E-mail don't have time to try to figure out what you mean. The Delete button is to the computer what the Circular File was to past generations.)
4. Be as correct in grammar and the conventions as you can.
5. Be polite. Say "thank you."

THE RISE AND FALL OF CASUAL FRIDAYS

When the custom of dressing down for work regularly became all the rage, it had a direct impact on the fashion industry, as you would expect, and on grammar, which you might not have guessed. Fortunately, the Grammar Lady was on the job to answer questions that arose over the use of the words *blue jeans.* Say a company wants to calls its casual Fridays "Jeans Day," should "jeans" be plural or possessive? Does the day belong to jeans, or is it just that many people are wearing them? It's not like Secretaries' Day; it is just Jeans Day. I personally would avoid the whole problem and stick with nice, plain, grammatically impeccable Casual Friday.

Now, on to the edifice complex. You'd think a CEO would know whether her headquarters (as in principal office) is singular or plural. But really this is a trick example. Use singular for one company's headquarters and plural for two or more companies' headquarters:

❋**Goofy Goof:** How about this one from a major corporation: A new campaign to market it's products.

- Bruder Company's headquarters is in Detroit.
- Bruder and Newton companies' headquarters are in Detroit.

Another frequent office disagreement involves sensitivity to the nuances of disability-related language. How to say in a brochure, for example, that offices are accessible to people with physical handicaps. *Handicapped-accessible* versus *handicap accessible*, neither of which seems quite correct. *Wheelchair accessible*? Here's my reasoning: *Handicap* is a noun and refers to the specific physical limitation—a person's blindness or paralysis, for example—but should never be used to refer to a person. Choosing between *handicapped-accessible* and *wheelchair-accessible* is dependent on what accommodations have been made for disabled persons. If what you're talking about are ramps and wider doorways, *wheelchair-accessible* sounds fine to me, since surely a person on crutches would understand that these features would help him or her as well. But if you have more extensive accommodations—Braille lettering or captioning for the hearing-impaired (as many museums now have), then *handicapped* would be the preferred (if somewhat undescriptive) term. If you are talking about something more elaborate than just the basics, I really think you should find a way to describe just what it is that is being offered in the way of access for disabled people, even if it means adding a footnote to your brochure.

HEARD AROUND THE WATER COOLER

Following is a roundup of commonly asked questions from the workplace.

What should the verb be in this sentence: "The confidence and trust of your colleagues *is/are* . . ." This comes up a lot. For some reason people want to combine two separate elements (confidence and trust) into a singular subject. However, it doesn't work; the sentence needs a plural verb: *are*.

What should the preposition be in this sentence: "I was glad to speak *with/to* you last week." The verb *speak with* usually indicates a conversation between colleagues. *Speak to* is often used by a superior to a subordinate: "I will speak to them about their behavior." If the person is going to address a group or give a lecture, use *to*. If there is going to be a conversation, use *with*.

What verb should we use here? "There *is/are* insufficient funds . . ." When *there* is at the beginning of the sentence, the subject is the noun on the other side of the verb, in this case *funds*. Since *funds* is plural, the verb must be *are*.

The use of *e.g.* and *i.e.* is a business-place bugaboo. The abbreviation *e.g.* means *for example* and is followed by an example of the preceding word or phrase. The abbreviation *i.e.* means *that is* and requires a paraphrase or rewording of what preceded it.

- A personal computer, e.g., an Apple Macintosh.
- A personal computer, i.e., a small computer for use by an individual.

Do you have trouble keeping *assure* and *ensure* separate? Try to think of *ensure* as an informal guarantee. *Assure* means to make someone confident about something: To *ensure* the success of our project, we worked very hard. I *assure* you that we will do our best.

Do you need *than* or *then* in this sentence: "We can wait no longer *than/then* two weeks from the date of . . ." *Than* is the connector that goes with comparatives such as *longer*. *Then* is an adverb that relates to time: "First, I'll do my work; *then* I'll go shopping."

WARNING: THESE WORDS MAY BE DANGEROUS TO YOUR REPORT

In case you are not proficient in bureaucratese, here is a cheat sheet of words you can use to sprinkle through reports. Pick one word from each column to make gobbledegook that sounds quite intelligent. No one will dare ask questions because all the words are comprehensible. It's the combination of adjectives and nouns that is nonsensical: *This procedure will result in integrated digital options and balanced optimal flexibility, which will improve the company's bottom line.*

parallel	management	flexibility
total	organizational	capability
systematized	monitored	mobility
integrated	reciprocal	programming
functional	digital	concept
responsive	optimal	contingency
balanced	options	

That's *my* bottom line.

GRAMMAR POINTS

addressing people in written correspondence
use of Esquire
Ms./Miss
U.S. Postal Service punctuation
cc = courtesy copy
identifying self on phone—formal
rudeness on phone
numbers and figures

numbers at the beginning of sentences
percent + verb agreement
SAMAN words + verb agreement
headquarters + verb agreement
handicap/ped accessible
speak to/with
there is/are
e.g./i.e.
assure/ensure
then/than
e-mail

MARY'S BEE

Find the misspelled words in the list below and correct them.

1. seperate

2. embarrass

3. pronounciation

4. accommodate

5. occurrence

6. concience

7. definately

8. indispensable

9. dependant

10. nickle

Typo of the Weak

From an earnest would-be private-sector contractor's proposal to the somber government, it will be duly deposited in our (burgeoning) Unfortunate Moment of Corporate Candor file.

We will demote ourselves to doing the job for the client.

Typo of the Weak

From a Philadelphia-area firm's marketing memo, it brings new meaning to the term *outhouse plumbing*.

The ultimate success of our product hinges on its perceived valve.

Typo of the Weak

A true flashback, eagerly furnished to me years ago during an informal "Scouts-honor, can you top that?" meeting of various been-there editors, by a colleague who swears she read this in a state or federal department or agency's brochure, or a news clipping. It will be duly deposited in our Who But They? file.

The census statistics were compiled by The Bureau of Copulation.

Chapter Six

The Home Front

When chatting with our friends and families, we often use informal and intimate language. That's fine and good and right. But even language used in informal settings should make sense grammatically. The home is the best place for children to learn standard English.

I define standard English as Walter Cronkite's English. Standard English means using the right noun with the right verb form. It demands the proper placement of modifiers. It eschews the word *ain't*. It lacks vulgarity. And it marks the speaker as educated and literate, in much the same way the use of nonstandard English correctly or not marks the speaker as unintelligent. People with a sound grasp of grammar may choose to break the rules occasionally. That's fine. But ignorance of grammar leaves people with no choice but to break the rules—sounding uneducated in the process.

The Grammar Lady understands that standard English is much harder to learn than nonstandard English is. Standard English boasts many (far too many, some of my students would say) irregular verbs. In nonstandard language, verb forms don't change. Take a look.

Standard	*Nonstandard*
I am not	I ain't
You are not	You ain't
He is not	He ain't
We are not	We ain't
You are not	You ain't
They are not	They ain't

The verb "ain't" doesn't change. The verb "ain't" is easy to use. But I feel that the value of sounding educated is well worth the time it takes to master the peculiarities of standard English. (Do my feelings on this matter really surprise anyone?)

Our daughter was born in 1978, a time when linguists hotly debated just how children acquire language skills. Poor kid, her early mutterings have been fodder for many lectures and seminars. Anyway, I decided immediately that we would not speak "baby talk" to her. Two factors influenced my decision. First, I believe it is hard enough for anyone to learn one version of English, let alone two. Second, I was far too old to sound so stupid.

Mary Beth started forming complete sentences quite late. In fact, I was worried that she wouldn't be able to communicate

---

WORRISOME WORD

OMNIVOROUS (ahm-NIV-er-us) adj. In the animal kingdom— eating both meat and vegetables. The prefix omni- means "all"; the root has to do with eating or consuming. You can tell from the context what these related words mean. *Most of the dinosaurs were herbivorous; T-Rex was carnivorous. Our dog is omnivorous—he will eat all meats and anything else with butter on it.* The figurative meaning of the word is avid—*she is an omnivorous reader of novels, plays, cereal boxes.*

with her nursery-school classmates. At two, she spoke in phrases incomprehensible to anyone but me. ("Diddens oss" for "mittens off," "dodo yips" for "potato chips," "yayats" for fancy.) Thankfully, by two and a half, she had graduated to complex sentences. ("If I go to sleep, I'll miss the sunset.")

Every child learns to speak at his own pace. In general, children start talking between the ages of eighteen months and two years. But the actual communication process begins much earlier than that. Babies make noises from birth. Adult reaction to those noises encourages children to repeat certain sounds and discard others. Kids learn by rote the phrases they hear over and over. ("Daddy went to work." "Three blind mice.") But almost inevitably the child will at some point come up with "Daddy goed to work," or "The mouses . . ."

At this point the child has begun to learn the rules of English grammar. He won't be able to tell you what they are, but you know the mental gears are turning because he has begun to apply these rules to words he has learned by rote.

If the child could express his thoughts, he might say something like this: "You add *d* to anything that happened yesterday: turn/turned, open/opened, go/goed. Or, You add *s* to make more than one: book/books, bear/bears, mouse/mouses."

At this point, parents must intervene—usually by repeating the child's statement back to him, only this time using the correct grammar. If the child asks for explanation, use the simplest reasoning possible: "It's just the way it is," you might say, or "It's irregular."

Children want to communicate and sometimes will go to great lengths to help you out. Here's a dialogue I once had with my daughter.

✼**Goofy Goof:** I'd like to add my two sense to the discussion.

MARY BETH: We forgot to go to the store and get a lollipop for me.

ME: What store?

MARY BETH: The doze store.

ME: What store?

MARY BETH: The doze store.

ME: I don't understand.

Finally, my daughter looked around, rubbed her hands on her pajamas and pointed to my shirt.

ME: Clothes?

MARY BETH: Yes.

The next time Mary Beth wanted to go to the clothes store, she pronounced the word pretty clearly. I never was able to determine exactly why she wanted to go to the clothes store to get a lollipop. After a while, I stopped asking.

Language acquisition is a process of trial and error. Sometimes, the parent feels as if she is taking two steps forward and one step back. But usually, questioning a child's use of incomprehensible language will help him focus his attention, and grasp for the right word, or right word form.

One day my daughter was helping me put the dishes away. She asked, "Where the knives go?"

ME: What?

MARY BETH: Where the knives go?

ME: What?

MARY BETH: Where *do* the knives go?

Don't get uptight about the grammatical errors your children make. Correct them when appropriate (meaning when they are old enough to understand your corrections) but don't allow your own stomach to knot. The mistakes your children make as youngsters are part of the learning process. They won't commit errors on purpose until they're teenagers and want to press your buttons.

Unfortunately for the budding grammarian, well-educated, hard-working teachers aren't the only people they'll encounter in primary school. Your children will meet up with a bunch of other tykes, as well. Their classmates will often use imperfect grammar—imperfect grammar that your kids will all too easily absorb.

When your child comes home from class using schoolyard slang, correct him immediately. Again, keep your explanation simple: "We don't talk like that in this house" should suffice. If you correct him often enough while he's still young enough to absorb it, he'll learn to keep schoolyard slang where it belongs—in the schoolyard.

The home is really the only place to tackle these language problems because kids don't talk much in the classroom, where they might otherwise be lovingly corrected by a caring teacher. Outside of school, other children will pressure your kids to sound just like everyone else. And everyone else is using bad grammar.

One reader complained about the ubiquitous use of the word *at.* Her children would regularly pose questions such as "Where's the book at?" She was only able to break them of this dreadful usage by consistently replying, "It's between the *A* and the *T.*" Only when her children rephrased the question did they receive a proper answer.

My reader may sound like a highly critical mother. Gentle Reader, she is not. She is simply a loving parent with the sense to recognize that her children's future success could be impeded if they walked around using nonstandard English. Her oldest daughter is now a fifth-grade teacher. She uses the same technique in her classroom that her mother employed in the home. Imitation is the most sincere form of flattery.

Teenagers, of course, often go through phases during which they use the worst grammar possible with the sole purpose of annoying their parents. My own daughter played this game. I was lucky, though. By the time she started spouting schoolyard slang, I realized she had her standard grammar down pat. I simply refused to rise to her bait.

I'VE HAD A PLENTIFUL SUFFICIENCY. I'M FULL, TOO.

One correspondent has two children, a little boy and a girl. When her son finishes his dinner, his sister will often ask, "All done?" My correspondent's husband always corrects his daughter, believing "All finished?" to be a more grammatically correct question. I think there must have been a rule like this at one time, at least in certain parts of the country, because the question arises frequently. However, today, the words "done" and "finished" can be used interchangeably in this context.

This issue, though, pales in comparison to the grammatically correct way of declining more food. Readers are often puzzled by the question of how to express one's satiety. Most people, when offered a second (or third or fourth, as the case may be) helping, reply, "No thanks, I'm full." This might sound acceptable but it reminds me of a young acquaintance who spent a few months in France. She thought she had sufficient command of French to make her way at age eighteen. If I had been her mother, she would have known she did not, but that is another story. At any rate, on the occasion of her first meal with a charming French family, she was asked if she'd care for a second helping of some delicious coq au vin. She replied, "Non, merci beaucoup. Je suis très pleine." The literal English translation of this sentence is "No, thank you very much. I'm quite full." Very polite, right? Unfortunately for my young friend, "full" in French means to be with child!

Southerners, meanwhile, seem to prefer the phrase "I'm stuffed." Why are Northerners full and Southerners stuffed? I don't actually know, but it's better than saying they're pregnant. I do know that there is a whole field in linguistics that deals with this. It's called sociolinguistics. I love sociolinguistics, but it's one reason I often disagree on points of grammar with colleagues. There is nothing wrong with the expression "I'm full" en famille or at a picnic, but my grandmother would have frowned mightily at her formal Sunday table.

Problems arise when the social situations and the appropriate grammar are mixed up. Some important humor is built on these things. *My Cousin Vinny* comes to mind.

That still leaves the question, How should you refuse an offer of more food? One reader suggested, "No, thank you. I've had a plentiful sufficiency; any more would be a superabundancy, obnoxious to my fastidious taste."

Is there a grammatically-and-politically correct phrase to denote one's feeling of satiety? Maybe there should be. We can deem this new phraseology "Grammetiquette."

IN THE KITCHEN WITH THE GRAMMAR LADY

It annoys one reader that recipes often order cooks to "slice (an object, say, an onion) thinly." The recipe is trying to instruct you to cut the onion into thin slices. But the adverb, thinly, describes how you slice, not the size of the onion bits resulting from your labors. To produce thin slices, you "slice them thin." This is a common grammar pattern: Subject + Verb + Object Complement. The complement refers to the object, as in "The gift made the child happy." You wouldn't say, "The gift made the child happily," and cookbook authors shouldn't write, "Chop the onion thinly." That much I know.

CONSIDER THE FROG

I didn't know the answer to one Hotline caller's question: how do you punctuate frogs legs before you eat them? It wasn't in the dictionary, so, being both resourceful and a fair cook, I looked it up in my cookbooks. Craig Claiborne has a recipe for "frogs' legs Provençale." James Beard agreed. Here's what I deduced: the frogs are plural, because you'd never eat only one set of legs, and possessive, because the legs definitely belong to the frog, so the apostrophe goes after the *s* in *frogs'*, n'est-ce pas?

Poor things.

In response to an inquiry about Scoville units (or Scovilles to the pepper in-crowd, known as chileheads, according to several readers) are a measure of heat in food, especially peppers. Scoville seems to have been a pharmacist in the early years of the twentieth century who was exploring the healing effects of capsaicin (cap-SAY-uh-sin), the substance that makes hot peppers hot, on such maladies as malaria, arthritis, shingles, and toothache. Bell peppers are the mildest at 0 Su and Habañero peppers the hottest at more than 100,000 Su. I'll bet you didn't expect to find that in a book about grammar.

Some friends were having a discussion about the following sentence. "He likes pancakes better than I/me." Both are grammatically possible. It depends on the meaning of the sentence. "He likes pancakes better than I (like pancakes)" or "He likes pancakes better than (he likes) me."

Real and really were troubling some folks. Is that real food? Is that really food? In the first sentence, real is an adjective modifying the noun food—Is that real food (or plastic)? In the second sentence, "really" is an adverb questioning the truth of the sentence. It could go at the beginning or the end of the sentence as well as before the noun. Suppose you're in a new culture and are served a plate of what looks like tree bark. You might say, "(Really) is that really food (really)?"

A reader thought I'd enjoy seeing the bottom of the take-out container from a local restaurant. "CAUTION. Not ovenable, for one time microwave reheating of food only." It's the first time she'd ever come across the word *ovenable,* but she knew exactly what it meant. People are certainly creative when it comes to language use.

LET THE GAMES BEGIN

At one caller's monthly Scrabble game, players use index cards to jot down their strategies. My pal had handed index cards to each player before the game. She said, "I'll pass the cards out now . . ."

✳ **Goofy Goof:** From a newspaper business column: Why should local, state, and federal bureaus and schools all be shut down when everybody else (except banks) are working.

Another player suggested that she had used incorrect grammar, adding that the phrase "pass the cards" would have been correct. I answered that, when playing Hearts, each player passes three cards facedown to another player. When the cards are dealt, they are passed out.

But wait, there's more. The Scrabble game produced the word *ungored*. The players found the word in an on-line unabridged dictionary. Who in his or her right mind would use such a reference for a serious Scrabble game anyway? The word's appearance there did not keep two English majors from flipping out over its use in the game. Die-hard Scrabble players have strict rules about what constitutes a word, but when a word can be made negative semantically it is done so by adding the prefix *un*. There was a popular song with the lyrics "unbreak my heart, uncry my tears," which seems poetic and interesting, but probably semantically impossible. "Ungored" does seem feasible—"The end of the bullfight found the bull unscathed and the matador ungored."

Personally, I found this subject a bit distasteful. Baseball is more up my sports alley than bullfighting. So I welcomed the question regarding the statement "I went to the ball game by myself." Is the pronoun "myself" reflexive or the object of the preposition? This is one of the three correct uses of reflexive pronouns—the other two are exemplified by "He has hurt himself," and "I signed the letter myself." Also, if you take "by myself" out of the "went to the ball game" sentence, you change its meaning.

WORRISOME WORD

OSTENTATIOUS (ahs-ten-TAY-shus) adj. Pretentious display, as of wealth or importance, in an attempt to impress others: an ostentatious dresser. *The huge house in the modest neighborhood was seen by everyone as ostentatious.*

The reflexive pronouns all end in *-self/-selves*. They always refer to someone mentioned previously or anticipated in the sentence. I asked the question *myself* (previous). He looked at *himself* in the mirror (anticipated).

- *I* want to do it *myself*.
- *He* wants to go by *himself*.
- On behalf of the Board and *myself*, I want to thank . . .
- *We*'ll get there by *ourselves*.
- Please make *yourself* at home. (Subject *you* is understood.)

Do not use the self words to avoid choosing between "I" and "me." They are only correct as used in the constructions above.

One of my youngest callers asked if the verb for her favorite game should be "jump roping" or "jumping rope." I replied that the verb always gets the *-ing* ending. One says "The boy was throwing up," not "The boy was throw upping." (Even the Ms. Manners of Grammar will occasionally use an inelegant analogy when it helps her get her point across.)

A couple of weeks ago, an official from a nearby town called to ask whether the signs they were going to put up to announce the boys/girls swimming teams should have apostrophes. "Of course they should," I answered. I guess I could have saved my breath, because they put up those signs sans apostrophes. The very next day. Naturally, a concerned resident (no, no, no, 'twas not I) called to complain. The same official told her that he had consulted an Expert who said that apostrophes were not necessary. He even went so far as to say that if the phrase is descriptive, the current trend is to omit the apostrophes. It is my opinion that the "current trend" derives from ignorance about when to use the apostrophe and intellectual laziness about finding out. I hereby challenge the officials to document this "current trend."

Need I say more? All right then, I will.

FAMILY MATTERS

Does the couple have one son and two daughters? No, no, no, the couple has one son and two daughters. The word *couple* is a collective noun (like *family, committee,* or *staff*) that can be used with a singular or plural verb depending on the context. If the couple is thought of as a single unit, it takes a singular verb: *Each couple was asked to bring a covered dish.* However, all the newspaper style books I consulted generally deem the word *couple* to be plural: *The couple were married in June.*

The issue of how couples identify themselves also perplexes some readers.

Let me tell you about my friends the Loxes. They had a sign made for the front of their house. The words *The Loxes* sat on the top line, with the couple's first names, Joe and Linda, sitting on the second. My friends suffered criticism from people who believed—quite wrongly (why are people always most vocal when they are wrong?) —that the couple should drop the *e*, and put an apostrophe between the *x* and the *s*. I advised Joe and Linda to stick to their guns. You'd only need an apostrophe if you used a noun after the possessive—i.e., if the sign had read The Loxes' House.

❋**Goofy Goof:** Here's a claim for a get-thin program: Stop Your Body's Fat-Producing Mechanism in Its' Tracks . . . Its'?!

MOMS AND DADS AND DADS AND MOMS

Callers frequently question the rule for capitalizing the words *mother* and *father* in a sentence. If the words can be replaced by a proper name, capitalize them. For example, *Of all the apple pies I've ever tasted, Mother's (Jane's) is the best.* Conversely, use a lowercase *m* or *f* if you cannot substitute a proper noun for the word *mother* or *father.* For example, you wouldn't say *Virtually all of today's Harrys and Janes agree that good grammar is good for children.* You would say *Virtually all of today's mothers and fathers agree . . .*

Someone called to ask whether it is correct to say "Tell your mother I was asking for her," or "Tell your mother I was asking after her." I suggested using the word *for* in formal situations when the speaker wishes to see the person immediately. The word *after* can be used in informal situations, when the speaker is merely inquiring after a person's well-being.

To further complicate the matter, one only "asks after" another person in the South. In the rest of the country, one "asks about" another. That's sociolinguistics again, in case you have forgotten already.

MY HUSBAND DON'T TALK SO GOOD

No matter how understanding a grammarian can be about her child's misuse of the language, an adult's mistakes can often drive her mad.

A reader wrote to tell me that her well-educated husband's poor grammar sounded, to her, like the startling crash of cymbals banged together in a quiet church. On a good day, she ignores it. On a bad day, she still ignores it—except she feels as if she is being pushed to some internal edge. The situation was exacerbated by her feeling that her husband was the only intelligent man in the universe who used the word *went* when he meant *gone*. She no longer felt quite so lonely after spending some time in front of the television. She watched an interview broadcast on national television, during which a lawyer said, "She should have went to her house instead of the store." (Of course, the subject of this sentence should have "gone home." Instead, she "went to" the store.)

My reader wondered whether the misuse of *went* and *gone* was a "tense" thing. "Sadly, no," I replied. "It's an ignorance thing." When school districts spend more than twenty years ignoring grammar, people grow ignorant of its proper use.

HANG IT UP

Questions about the proper use of the words *hang* and *hung* crop up so frequently that I sometimes fret. After all, the Grammar Lady does not wish to serve the vigilante community. Here are examples of correct/incorrect usage.

Incorrect

- My boyfriend got angry and hanged up on me.
- I hanged the laundry on Thursday.
- The murderer was hung at midnight.

Correct

- My boyfriend got angry and hung up on me.
- I hung the laundry on Thursday.
- The murderer was hanged at midnight.

BE ALERT! LERTS ARE VERY POPULAR

A waitress greeted a gentleman who entered the restaurant with "Hi, Joe, are you being have?" She pronounced "have" to rhyme with "gave." A caller asked me what this could possibly mean. I had no idea, so I researched the word *have*. After a few hours of digging, reading only what you'd expect about the common use of the verb "to have," the Grammar Lady still had no idea. So I did what I often do in a pinch—I asked my readers. (By now you're no doubt wondering why I included this in a chapter called "The Home Front." Patience.)

The replies trickled in. Apparently, it's a joke shared in homes across the country. The mother says, "Johnny, behave!" Johnny replies, "I am being have," or "I'm very have." So now the question becomes, how funny is that?

IN THE END

Recently while walking through a cemetery, I noticed that many of the newer monuments have inscriptions on the backs describing the deceased's relationship to immediate family members (probably to be helpful for future generations in tracing their genealogical lineage). I noticed that some monuments were in-scribed like this: *Son of Dick and Jane. Brother to Tom, Dick, and Harry.* Are the words *of* and *to* used correctly in these two cases, or should the chiseler inscribe *of* in all cases? The older phrase would be "Son to" and "Brother to." I think that today, people should use the word *of.* Consistency, above all!

GRAMMAR POINTS

should have + past participle
couple—collective noun
slice + adj/adv
jump rope verb
apostrophe in name sign
finished eating
capitalization of Mother/Father
like as filler word
"being have"
satiation at dinner
ask for/after
where's it at?
pass (out) cards
response to negative question
myself
thank you—possessive
hanged/hung
un- as a prefix
brother of/to

MARY'S BEE

Here's a multiple-choice food theme quiz. I defy you to complete it before you rush off to find a snack!

1. Nut or fruit-filled candy
    nougate / nougat / nugat

2. Mexican peppers
    jalapeño / jalapenno / jallapeño

3. Clear soup
    consomé / consummé / consommé

4. Ground vegetables fried in patties
    falafel / felafal / falafell

5. Spicy Chinese cooking
    czechuan / Szechuan / Sechzuan

6. Espresso with milk
    capuccino / cappuccino / cappucino

7. Having a protein found in wheat flour
    glutinous / gluitinous / glutenous

8. Appetizers
    hor d'ovres / hors d'ouvres / hors d'oeuvres

9. Dish of beans and corn
    succotash / sucotash / succotache

10. Support for hot dish
    trivette / tryvet / trivet

11. Small cabbage-type vegetable
    kolrabi / kohlrabi / kohlrabe

12. Sugary brown syrup
    molasses / molassas / molasas

13. Spice from tree bark
    cinamon / cinammon / cinnamon

14. Type of turnip
    rutabaga / rootabaga / rootibaga

15. Fermented cherry
    mareschino / marraschino / maraschino

Typo of the Weak

From a hand written instruction tag affixed to a National Park–area guest cabin's heater. And all along we thought only laughing gas was irreverent.

Warning: This pressurized metal container contains profane gas.

Typo of the Weak

From a French cookbook. And we thought they were more tolerant of harmless flirtations over there. Mon Dieu!

Fry the coquette in deep fat.

Typo of the Weak

From a Los Angeles–based aerospace company's poop sheet; it brings new meaning to the terms "fuel efficiency" and "fast-food."

The rocket lunched precisely on schedule.

WORRISOME WORD

ENIGMATIC (ehn-ig-MAT-ic/ee-nig) adj. Mysterious. *People say that the Mona Lisa has an enigmatic smile.*

Chapter Seven

Polishing the Apple

A recent *Parade* magazine poll asked students nationwide "How we can make our schools better?" One of the more thoughtful responses: "I wish my teachers would let us chew gum in class. Most of us are mature enough not to stick it on the bottom of the desk." I did not allow students to chew gum in my classroom either, but maturity was not the issue. The students thought I didn't allow gum because it would interfere with their French accents, but there was a more esthetic reason. Have you ever watched cows chewing their cuds? I rest my case.

It's 8:07 on a Sunday morning in wintry January. A car with a security system begins to honk—every five seconds for five minutes. All sleep has been dispelled for the duration. So I begin to read *The Force upon the Plain* and less than a half hour later, the honking starts again. Is it some kind of omen about reading this book? Then I learn on page seventy-one that the Militia of Montana has issued some of its instructions in diagramed sentences. If I had reservations about the usefulness of diagraming as a teaching tool, the question is now settled. It is clear that diagraming is a right-wing conspiracy to prevent kids from learning English grammar.

A SMALL DIAGRAMING DIGRESSION

By the way, does anyone know why diagraming is usually spelled with two em's? Well, according to Mr. Webster, the spelling with one em is preferred; and the two-em version is labeled "esp. Brit." Since the single-em version is in accord with a very useful spelling rule, we'll use it even though the spell checker is going to have a problem.

What's the rule? I thought you'd never ask.

Doubling the final consonant of the base word. If a one-syllable word ends in a single consonant (knit), preceded by a single vowel (*i*), the final consonant (*t*) is doubled when the suffix begins with a vowel (*er* makes knitter). Are you with me? Examples: run + er = runner, hot + er = hotter. But rain + ed = rained, because there are *two* vowels before the consonant.

In a two-syllable (or longer) word with the same spelling pattern at the end (a single consonant preceded by a single vowel), listen to the stress. If the stress is on the last syllable, double the final consonant. If the stress is on any other syllable, the consonant is not doubled. Let's look at two words commonly misspelled when suffixes are added: occur and focus. The ending spellings fit the rule, but the stress is on the second syllable in oc-CUR, so we double the *r*—occurred, occurring. The stress is on the first syllable of FO-cus, so we don't double the *s*—focused, focusing. The word

---

WORRISOME WORD

OSTENSIBLE (ah-STEN-suh-bull) adj. Seeming to be other than is really the case; pretending. *Ms. Green was the ostensible leader; in fact, the decisions were made by a secret group of wealthy financiers.*

DIE-uh-gram has the same spelling pattern but the stress is on the first syllable. Hence, no double em.

DIAGRAMING — SERIOUSLY

I was just kidding about the conspiracy theory, but there *is* a serious controversy raging regarding diagraming. People who find it easy usually find it useful and defend it as a teaching tool. No one is neutral on this; people are fervently for or against the practice. Believe me, I should know. After an Associated Press interview appeared in which I was quoted as saying something somewhat uncomplimentary about diagraming sentences, I was deluged with calls on my own toll-free Grammar Hotline for my down-with-diagraming attitude. One woman called twice saying I probably had not had a very good teacher.

People who didn't get diagraming when it was taught to them in school have painful memories of the struggle and are surprised (and happy) to hear my view. When I mentioned this to my husband he muttered, "I hated diagraming. I was tutored in it by Mrs. Core." He doesn't remember how old he was when he underwent this tutelage, but he remembers how awful it was as well as the poor woman's name.

I was one of those nerdy kids who *liked* to diagram sentences because it was easy. As I think about it I'm not sure it taught me anything much about English grammar. Most people my age had to take foreign languages, and that's how I learned English grammar because the approach used to teach foreign languages at the time was grammar translation. I became a grammar maven, however, when I taught non-English speakers. They ask totally off-the-wall questions and expect the English-speaking teacher to know the answers.

Speaking of off the wall, did you see the end of the Broncos–Jets championship game when Greg Gumbel commented on John Elway's game: "John Elway, getting all the platitudes and congratulations he so richly deserves . . ." I didn't know someone could deserve platitudes. Care to diagram that, Greg? (Oh no, the spell checker just changed Greg's last name to Gumboil and John's to Always. Have to be careful with that device.)

The diagraming practice is still alive and well in the public schools, however. At least once a week I get a question about it from a teacher or a student (or a parent) suffering with homework. I even had a call from a college student who had to diagram sentences for his English 101 course. That's preposterous.

For the sake of argument, which I dearly love, let's say in the real world, diagraming vanishes from the schools. How are the kids to learn grammar, you ask? Do I have an answer for that? You bet!

When our daughter was in elementary school, the children did the same boring grammar exercises year after year with more complex sentences added to the regimen as the kids learned to read better. Suppose math were taught this way and the students were still doing math facts up through eighth grade? The teachers and the students would be just as sick of math facts as they are of English grammar. Math facts are memorized early so people can learn more advanced math. Grammar facts should be handled in exactly the same way. Children should learn the basics (identifying parts of speech, tenses, the functions of words in sentences) by third grade while they are learning to read. In fact, grammar instruction should be part of the learning-to-read process. After third grade

❋**Goofy Goof:** Here is a statement from the station manager of one of the branch offices of the U.S. Postal Service. "The United States Postal Service has a long history of service to our customers. I, and the employees of the XXX Branch, are improving on this history by establishing your satisfaction as our number one concern."

the function of grammar in the classroom should be to facilitate writing and more advanced reading. At no time should grammar be taught in a vacuum.

AND NOW FOR SOMETHING COMPLETELY SPECIFIC

If you're still not convinced that diagraming should be thrown out with the bathwater, let me share a couple of ideas I've shared with teachers over the years.

One teacher asked how to help his third grade students learn subject-verb agreement. My idea about teaching grammar is always the same and always different. Find a story that rivets students to their chairs or has them jumping for joy. Read it with all the drama you can muster. (I think kids this age are into gore, and Halloween was just around the corner.) Then make worksheets based on the story using sentences that have different subject and verb combinations. Have the students do more than just read the sentences. Ask them to think about why the author chose that specific verb and so on. Then they can write a story in the same genre. If the kids speak standard English, they won't have much trouble about verb agreement. If they don't, you can refer them to the appropriate sentences from the story.

Another teacher had a fourth grade class learning to write dialogue for a book they were producing. For many years the school officials hadn't paid much attention to the mechanics and punctuation of dialogue. The parents were concerned. The teacher wanted me to suggest a reference manual that she could use, so the students could look up the rules for themselves. It pleased me to no end that the parents were concerned. It may be that the parents are the products of the nonchalant attitude about teaching English for the past twenty years, and they realize now how hard it is to learn these details later on. In any case, most grammar books are pretty boring and don't contain all the specific questions the students have. I suggested she provide the students with examples of good, well-edited children's literature that includes dialogue material and let them deduce the punctuation for themselves as a class exercise.

This suggestion was met with one of the strongest tongue lashings I have ever received.

I was astonished, if not appalled, by your response to the fourth-grade teacher who asked you to recommend a grammar reference manual. In my work, I am constantly exposed to written legal briefs and memoranda. More often than not, the writers have never learned the first thing about grammar, even though they have all been through twelve years of public school, four years of college, and three years of graduate school. Many of them don't know how to write a complete sentence, much less how to punctuate it properly. If someone with this much education cannot follow rules of punctuation, how can fourth graders be expected to "deduce the punctuation for themselves" as you suggest? By allowing the students to "deduce for themselves" rather than teaching the basic grammar rules, we are doing a disservice to those students. When they arrive in the real world of work, they will not be as capable and employable as people who have learned proper punctuation and other grammar rules.

Don't worry, although this letter might appear persuasive, I was equal to the task of rising to the occasion of a pithy response:

My condolences for your working conditions, but you make my point very well. The people you work with have undergone traditional methods of learning grammar and still don't know it. Are they not capable and gainfully employed? Most people find grammar and punctuation boring because for the most part it is taught that way year after mind-numbing year. The teacher in question wanted a reference to teach the students how to punctuate dialogue. There is an excellent body of good literature for students of this age. If the teacher uses something that engages the students' attention as well as illustrates the types of punctuation to be taught, two things are accomplished: the students see that punctuation has a real-life use, and they have learned the lesson in a new and different way. Perhaps they will retain their knowledge past the end of the year.

THE READING CONTROVERSY: PHONICS VERSUS WHOLE LANGUAGE

There are generally two schools of thought on teaching reading, and they go in and out of fashion, as do most educational fads. One is called "phonics," in which the students learn the sounds of the letters and sound out words. Detractors of this method point out that English has a very bad fit between the spelling and the sounds (trough, although, bough) and advocate a method where the students look at the word, hear it, and say it. It used to be called "look-say" but in this reincarnation it is referred to as "whole language." The problem is that each method on its own will not produce successful readers. I once visited a third grade class, for the purpose of exploring why the reading scores were down. The children greeted me with an astonishing demonstration of their phonics skills. My first recommendation was that third grade was much too late to be doing phonics.

Here's a little doggerel to illustrate:

I love this country very much, and I plan to stay.
But students learning English may have reason for dismay.
Why is there an *s* in island, and why an *h* in school?
Who put *p* in psychology? Who made up that rule?
Why can't we spell by sound—let RIME spell rhyme.
Why can't we make it simple—like TIME spells time.
Then we have the homonyms—enough to make one cry.
When choosing whether kings do rain or reign falls from the
sky.
Is it the bored of education or are we so board we sigh?
Do we yearn for piece on earth or for a peace of pie?
The logic for this confusion is nowhere to be found.
It isn't at all like math where rules are clear and sound.
The reason for this confusion cannot be found by me.
I'd rather take a math test than face a spelling bee.

On the other hand, students taught only the whole language method often turn out to be bad spellers. My husband is a good example. We both went to school at the same time in upstate New York, but he lived near Albany, the capital and home of a large teacher's college that produced teachers trained in the latest methods. At the time, the look-say (whole language) method was newly popular, and the schools nearest the source got new things first. By the time it reached midstate, I had already learned to read and spell using the old phonics approach. One day, not too long ago, my husband asked me where Canandaigua was—he was reading an article about a summer conference in the paper. When I later looked at the article, I noticed it was about Chatauqua. It's a miracle he doesn't get lost more often. Maybe that's why he prefers to fly his airplane rather than struggle with highway signage. When you're hundreds of miles in the air, there's no spelling confusion.

My not really radical proposal is to combine the two methods: teach phonics where the sound and the symbols fit and whole language where they don't. The consonant letters are not much of a problem, but the five vowel letters have to take care of a dozen or more sounds. Still, it can be done. Here is an example from one of my very own previously published books:

There are five basic spelling patterns for the long *a* sound in the word *ape*, represented by these words:

1. game/safe (letter *a* + consonant + *e*)
2. baby/nation (letter *a* + consonant + vowel)
3. air/fail (letter combination *ai*)
4. day/pay (letter combination *ay*)
5. eight/weigh (letter combination *ei*)

Here are some words that have the same sound but not the same pattern. They have to be memorized with this sound:

1. able/taste
2. great/wear
3. their/veil
4. there/where
5. they/obey
6. bury/very

(Words with the *ei* combination can be pronounced *ee* as in *receive* or *ai* as in *height*. These words would be presented with those sounds.)

Then there are words that don't follow *any* rules. We call them

❉**Goofy Goof:** "For all intensive purposes."

"tough ones" because those two words exemplify the category. Traditionally they are called "sight words" and must be learned by the whole language technique. One for this sound is *ache*.

In fact, the students must learn the meaning of the words as they are learning the spellings; otherwise spelling becomes a mechanical task, and nothing is learned. As soon as the children master how to sound out words, probably by the end of first grade, phonics can—and should—be discarded. The children then have a tool that they can use the rest of their lives when they come across new words.

One woman called to ask for a reference to help her son, who was having a lot of trouble with spelling. I should have asked if her son had had any phonics training. It would have made a difference in what I recommended. Without having more information about the specific problems, it is impossible to recommend any single book, but here are a few suggestions for making a choice. The best bets are probably going to be the older reference books in the library and in secondhand bookstores. The books are often old and dusty and sometimes hard to read, but they contain the old-time rules. Start in the reference section of the bookstore or library. Choose a book that is organized according to some principle, not simply an alphabetical list of difficult words. Some are organized according to the similarities in the sounds. For example: *wait, weight, late* might be grouped together as three different spellings of the same vowel sound. Others are organized according to spelling patterns. Others use parts of speech or word parts (prefixes, suffixes) as organizers. Choose the one that makes sense to you and that addresses the specific problems you or your child has with spelling. Exercises and tests are useful; the answers should be available, either at the back of the book or the bottom of the page. The lessons should be short, and, if at all possible, fun. Learning to spell correctly is basically tedious; so the more interesting the material, the easier it will be.

CORRECTNESS IN CLASS

I heard from a mother whose children were having a terrible time with spelling in elementary school. What made it worse was that their teachers didn't seem to care. They believed that if they fussed about spelling, they would "harm the children's self-esteem." The mom thought it would be worse for her children's self-esteem to get into the real world and not be able to spell.

I'm here to tell you that you cannot give someone self-esteem. Self-esteem comes with doing a job well and being honestly praised for it, and as a result feeling good about oneself. If children are not corrected, how will they know if they have done something right or wrong?

When children speak another language or a nonstandard variety of English, it is the responsibility of the school to insist that standard English is the currency of the school and provide models and opportunities to learn it. When the school and the teachers set standards and expect the students to meet them, they will.

I understand it is very difficult for teachers to insist on a language standard without seeming to reject the home or background of the child. But this is not a problem when the language is not English. We need to establish and respect both Home Language and School Language. What the family speaks at home is not the business of the school (don't ask; don't tell). What everyone speaks at school is the standard that will be needed later for wider communication in society—getting and keeping jobs. It needs to start at the earliest grades and continue to graduation.

A comment on the notion that communication is all and correctness doesn't matter. The increasing number of calls and letters to my Grammar Hotline convinces me that many people *do* care about correctness. The passionate discussions I hear on talk radio persuade me that the pendulum is swinging back. Soon school-children will be memorizing parts of speech again. The trend is encouraging, but I shudder to think of the boring grammar classes the kids will have to endure.

A man called to say his granddaughter had a cheer at school that went "Don't mess with us no more." He told her it should be "Don't mess with us anymore." The granddaughter said he was wrong because her teacher said it was right. He said that the teacher needed to restudy the English language. This issue has come up on many occasions—the misuse of language unhindered by the school personnel. My position has always been that the teachers should provide accurate models of language use and should provide correction where needed. An individual does not usually become completely proficient in the use of the native language until early adulthood; and even after that, there is always evolution in a living language. A love of correctness and accuracy is a lasting gift that all teachers should try to provide.

In a book report, a student used the exact spelling from the book for the names of two gangs. The protagonist's gang was always referred to without a capital letter, so he spelled it that way in his report. The teacher took points off, even after she was shown the examples from the book. She said he should have known better. His mother wondered what he should have done. It's too bad the teacher didn't use the opportunity to teach her students what to do in this situation. When quoting something that seems strange in some way, the writer puts (sic) after the word or phrase. It's a Latin word meaning "so," and it tells the reader that the quoted material appears exactly as the original author wrote it. The boy should be commended, not penalized, for trying to be accurate.

Then there were the parents who sent their son to an expensive private school to find that the English teacher was "correcting" their son's papers—incorrectly. It turns out that English was not her native language. I didn't ask where the teacher was from, but a lot of people think a foreign accent, especially a French one, is very classy. I'd be arranging a change of schools.

A student complained that her English teacher frequently used the expression "that's how come I made you do this or that." She wondered about the use of the phrase "how come." She thought the word *why* should have been used. This is a very common question: *Why did he skip school on Friday?* versus *How come he skipped school on Friday?* The *Random House Unabridged Dictionary* lists "how come," meaning "why," as informal, which means that it is more normally used in speech than writing and that it is used among friends when an informal language style is appropriate. Many teachers like to use informal language in the classroom to indicate to the students that they are friendly and accessible, so that may explain the teacher's usage. I think the use of the phrase "how come" is fine in friendly or familial situations, but I would use "why" in written or formal milieus.

I'm really not as strict as I might appear. I am often amused by language variations that make purists cringe. However, I think it is a teacher's responsibility (all teachers—not just the English teachers) to be a role model for students in their language use. If a teacher is going to use informal language such as this, it should be acknowledged so the students know how to interpret it.

This sentence was in a letter mailed to a school: ". . . show the educators how fun X can be." The expression "It was so fun" is very popular with teenagers, but it is not correct in standard language. "Fun" is a noun; we need an adjective—funny, happy, cool—in its place. The sentence might also be fixed by adding "much"; "show how much fun X can be."

(I wonder why fixed is not spelled with two *x*s. It is yet another exception to the rule at the beginning of this chapter. English is such an endearing language, don't you agree?)

A copyeditor found the following ubiquitous error in the director of curriculum's interview concerning awards for a school's "excellence in writing": "If the students would have had to . . ." The editor changed it to "If the students had been required to . . ." thus sparing the school much embarrassment. Other possibilities occurred to him: "Had the students had to . . ." or "Had the students been required to . . ." The first choice was probably best because the others are very formal patterns in speech. Another choice would have been "If the students had had to . . . ," which simply corrects the grammar without changing the verb. This error puzzles me because I can't understand the source except perhaps lack of instruction in the advanced grammar patterns.

Another possibility just occurred to me—possibly the contraction *'d*, which is sometimes *had* (I'd gone) and sometimes *would* (I'd go) is at the heart of this. It requires investigation. Maybe my next book will be by Mary Newton Bruder a.k.a. The Grammar Sleuth.

COMMON QUESTIONS FROM TEACHERS AND STUDENTS

One teacher had never heard of the rule that says inanimate objects do not take the *'s* possessive form. Apparently she's not alone.

WORRISOME WORD

ESOTERIC (es-uh-TARE-ik) adj. Known by or meant for people with special interest or knowledge. Synonyms: recondite; arcane; enigmatic. Note that the term is relative; what seems esoteric to some people is everyday information for people in the special field. *He tried to impress us with the esoteric terminology of quantum physics, but everyone got bored. International students are often confused by the esoteric Biblical references in Western literature.*

Quirk and Greenbaum, authors of *A Concise Grammar of Contemporary English*, discuss the difficulty in knowing when to use *of the* or *'s* (the cover of the book/the book's cover), but conclude that generally *'s* is used with "animate nouns, in particular persons and animals with personal gender characteristics." In some cases we can use either pattern: the smallest child's games/the games of the smallest child. However, the two are not always interchangeable: the color of the paper, but not the paper's color.

Many students want to know why people say that "ain't" is not a word when it is in the dictionary. Time for a little history lesson. Until the 1970s dictionaries were the "keepers" of correct language. If something was "in the dictionary" it had the seal of approval. Teachers could say "ain't" is not in the dictionary—it's not a word. (These are the people who say it now, probably—not teachers, per se, but people used to this older dictionary style.) In the early 1960s *Webster's Third Unabridged* made a radical change and included everything—proper or not—along with usage notes on the questionable words and idioms. This outraged people who used the dictionary as a standard of language use and eased the minds of people who knew that ain't certainly *is* a word that has a preferred spelling and meanings. So now people can no longer depend solely on the dictionary, and it makes them nervous.

Students often ask the difference between "domestic animals" and "domesticated animals." "Domestic" designates cats and dogs and animals that live with the family. "Domesticated" refers to cattle, horses, and sheep.

A teacher needed help explaining commas to one of her bright seven-year-old students. She had taught her a comma can show a short pause in a sentence, shorter than a period. The girl sometimes put a comma in a long sentence when she had to take a breath in reading it. I recommended the teacher teach her the rules—there aren't that many, and running out of breath isn't one of them. I suggested that she use her reading material, find the commas in the selection, and discuss why they are used.

RULES FOR COMMAS

Conventional Uses

Dates. The day of the week is separated from the month and the month from the year; the current trend is to omit the comma after the year. *On Monday, February 22, 1996 we paid off the mortgage.* If only the month and year are given, no comma is needed. *In June 1998 we leave for Europe.*

Addresses. Use a comma between the city and the state. *The company is located in Detroit, Michigan.* In a line of text separate all items in an address. *They now live at 12 Thoreau Court, Concord, Massachusetts.*

Openings. In friendly letters and closings in letters of all kinds. Example: Dear Mary Ann, . . . Sincerely, The Grammar Lady.

Titles. Achieved titles are separated from the name—Judith Doe, Ph.D. There is no comma between a name and the abbreviations Jr., Sr., and numerals (III, IV) because these designations are necessary to the identification of the individual.

Direct address. You know, Mr. President, I think we should . . .

Separating Items in a Series

The basic rule is to separate more than two items in a series by commas. There is disagreement among the authorities about whether to include a comma before the conjunctions *and, or*. Two major journalistic style manuals advise omitting the comma; my unabridged dictionary says it's optional; my trusted grammar book says to include it. Because I am a creature of language habit, I continue using a comma in this place unless it affects the meaning of the sentence. For example: *The estate was divided by Tom, Dick, Jean and Harry.* Without the comma after Jean, there are three parts to the inheritance; with the comma, there are four. Grammar matters.

Items that are pairs of words are set off as one item in a series. *I had ham and eggs, toast, coffee, and juice for breakfast.*

Joining Clauses

When two independent clauses (both have a subject and a verb and each can stand alone as a sentence) are connected by the conjunctions *and, but*, or, *nor*, there is a comma before the conjunction.

- The meeting was dull at first, but then the Director fired everyone.
- We submitted the report, and they took months to respond.
- Mr. Jones will report to work on time in the future, or he will find himself without a job.

If the clauses are very short, no comma is needed. *You take the bike and I'll use the skates.*

If one of the clauses has a comma included in it, the two are separated by a semicolon. *We invited the Joneses, the Perrys, the Newtons, and the Grays; but everyone was too sick to enjoy the rich food.*

Setting off Elements at the Beginning of a Sentence

1. Words like *yes, no, well* are set off by a comma at the beginning of a sentence. *Yes, we've come to a time in history . . .*

2. Introductory phrases (phrases do not contain both a subject and a verb). *Believing in free market forces, our company has just . . . At the end of a long road through tall iron gates, you will find . . .*

3. Introductory clauses are set off by a comma. *When you and your family travel to Detroit, please plan . . . If you have excess funds at the end of the fiscal year, we will discuss . . .* Note: These clauses are not set off if they come at the end of the sentence. *We will discuss it if there are excess . . .*

Separating Nonessential (Parenthetical) Elements

Commas are used to set off nonessential (nonrestrictive) material from a sentence. The material, usually associated with a noun, is not necessary for the identification of the noun.

- Mr. Jones, formerly with XYZ Corp., has taken a new position with ABC.
- The new church, which is nearly completed, will have the first service next week.
- Mr. J., the new sixth grade teacher, seems to be enjoying his work.

Material that is essential (restrictive) to the identification of the noun is not set off by commas. *The man who called on the phone wanted to know about commas. Is this the ring that Bill gave you?*

Sometimes a clause can be interpreted as either essential or non-essential depending on the context. *They took the checks to the teller, who was just finishing a break.* (There was only one teller. The clause is nonessential.) *They took the checks to the teller who was just finishing a break.* (There were several tellers. The clause is essential.)

A student asked when to put a comma between adjectives in a series. There is a natural sequence of descriptive adjectives that does not require commas: *two lovely large old red wool scarves.* The sequence seems to be something like: number + general description + size + age + color + noun. If we use more than one adjective from the same category or if the categories are out of order, we seem to need commas: *smaller, cheaper, better spacecraft.*

Someone stated that there is no superlative form to the word *new,* despite its common use in the media. An item is either new or it is not—newer or newest would imply an item of the future, not the recent past. However, I do not think "new" has the absolute sense as does "unique." For example, if I buy a 1969 Impala, it is new to me; then if I buy a 1962 Vette, it is the newer car in my fleet. Each addition is the newest one.

In working with subject-verb agreement problems with high school juniors, a teacher was stumped by the following sentence: "This is not the only house that *needs/need* repair. The only choices for antecedents were singular (*this* and *house*) therefore the verb is singular—needs. But the idea of the sentence is that more than one house must be repaired, so why shouldn't the verb be plural? I must admit to a moment's loss as to what to say in answer to this question. In all the years I have been teaching there has never been one like it. Here goes: Grammar works at the sentence level. Semantics and philosophy take care of ideas. Please let me digress a bit to say that perhaps this is at the heart of our current language chaos. Grammar pertains to the sentence at hand and nothing more.

ON KNOWING GRAMMAR RULES

This question comes up very frequently, and people often apologize because they can't remember the rule. "If I *was/were* in Paris . . . " The short answer is, When the condition is not real, use "were," especially in writing, when more formal language is appropriate.

The long answer addresses the linguistic insecurity of English speakers, especially speakers of American English. When I am introduced to someone new as "the Grammar Lady," I cringe, because in many cases the new people won't speak to me for fear of "saying something wrong." For the most part people do not often make mistakes in speech, and people who do need not be afraid of the Grammar Lady's wrath. (My mother taught me to be polite.) People who write for public consumption and make mistakes are not excused. It puzzles me, however, that people think they should remember esoteric rules of grammar that refer mostly to writing and that are relatively unused. Are people ashamed because they can't

---

WORRISOME WORD

DISINGENUOUS (dis-in-JEN-you-us) adj. Lacking in frankness, candor, or sincerity; insincere; slightly dishonest and untruthful. (This is a very polite way of calling someone a liar.) *Pardon me, Senator, but that last statement strikes me as somewhat disingenuous. The politician's explanation for the excessive junkets seemed disingenuous to the voters, who elected his opponent at the next opportunity.*

remember how to solve problems with quadratic equations? The reason I know the details is that I have an advanced degree in linguistics and have taught English to international students for many years. Even then I have a vast library of reference texts to look up the answers to unusual questions. Native speakers of most languages do not know the details of the grammar of their language. I have worked with groups of Argentine, Slovak, Bulgarian, and many other teachers of English who know much more about English grammar than they do of their native language. So, stop apologizing; what's important is that a person cares to be correct and recognizes when there is a question.

For example, how can we tell if a word is a noun, and why do we want to? The answer to this question falls under the need-to-know category, similar to how I imagine the CIA decides who should be told there has been a terrorist threat. In general, it is not really necessary for competent native speakers of a language to know the nitty-gritty details of their language. We can read, write, and understand without reference to this information. On the other hand, there are times when we need to know, such as deciding which words to capitalize in the title of a document (nouns, verbs, adjectives, and adverbs) or working a crossword puzzle. Learning foreign languages is easier if we know the basic terms of grammar. So, let's say we need to know sometimes, and it's embarrassing not to know; what do we do?

Standard grammar texts have a definition that goes something like this: A noun is a word used to name a person, place, or thing. Then nouns are further classified as common or proper, abstract or concrete, and collective. At this point the terminology overwhelms most people. Try this instead.

1. Most nouns can be counted: one house/two houses; one mouse/two mice.
2. But not all: milk, news, scissors. Most nouns can fit in this

frame: The *noun* is/are . . . The milk is cold. The news is bad. The scissors are sharp.

3. But not all: haste, America. Then try this frame: *Noun* is . . . Haste is necessary. America is in trouble.

To summarize, we need a new way to talk about language that is easier to teach and learn and remember how it works to communicate our ideas effectively. I'll be working on it.

A FEW SPELLING TIPS FOR GOOD MEASURE

Here's a trick for remembering stationery/ary: You use stationEry to write lEttErs. Here's another one. StationEry goes into the Envelope.

Many people have trouble knowing whether words are spelled with "able" or "ible." What about preempti/able? It's preemptible. These suffixes are tricky, and this hint won't always work; but try to think of a related word with a different suffix: preempt/preemptive. The vowel *a/i* will usually be the same as able/ible.

Words that end in "sede," "ceed," and "cede" cause all kinds of spelling mischief. There is not really a rule, but there are so few of these words that they are easily memorized. Only one word ends in "sede": supersede. Three end in "ceed": succeed, exceed, and proceed. The others with the same sound end in "cede." For example, concede, recede, precede.

❋ **Goofy Goof:** A few years ago, lost on back roads, I saw this sign on the lawn of a house: Antiques—New and Old.

ONE LAST QUESTION

A home-schooling mom called to ask for a reference for her thirteen-year-old son, who had finished the six or so levels of grammar workbooks. I told her that if he had finished that many levels of grammar workbooks, he should know all the grammar he needed and should move on to reading and writing compositions. She replied, "Well, he don't."

ON SECOND THOUGHT . . . ONE MORE LAST COMMENT

A man wrote that he was not an expert in the language, but he will never forget Sr. M. Francesca and her rule—2001 is a single whole number, one word: two thousand one. No "and" or you would flunk Sr. M. Francesca's math class. It seems fitting for this to be the last word, at least on this subject.

Grammar Points

spelling rule—doubling final consonant
diagraming sentences
grammar and learning foreign languages
teaching subject-verb agreement
learning punctuation
teaching reading
teaching spelling
correctness in school
standard/nonstandard English
home/school language

how come/why
fun as adjective
if + past perfect
tips
   stationEry
   able/ible
   parts of speech
   sede/ceed/cede
possessive of inanimate objects
saying a number
comma in series before *and*
ain't
domestic/ated
teaching commas
comma rules
series of adjectives
new/er/est
on knowing grammar rules

PERFECTLY PUNCTUATED

Punctuate the following sentences:

1. Where were you on Friday October 13 1985 at 10 o'clock in the morning?

2. The policy covers collision liability property damage and personal injury.

3. Jane Morgan Esq. will address the group this month.

4. You always seem to know what to do Bill.

5. Introducing herself to all the guests she made her way toward the door.

6. After you have completed the tape please send it to my attention.

7. We will discuss this further when you have time.

8. Take as long as you need with this report but we need it by the end of the day.

9. After conducting a national poll the researchers concluded that the prices of bananas are too high in our area and they have recommended that we should boycott all merchants who have bananas.

10. If you hear of a good new dictionary please let me know.

PERFECTLY PUNCTUATED

Where do you put commas in the following sentences? There, I gave you a big hint.

1. The man asked for coffee toast and ham and eggs.

2. New York Maryland Pennsylvania and Ohio are in the same region.

3. The policy covers collision liability and property damage.

4. Apples peaches pears and grapes are available now.

5. We fought cried laughed and sang.

Typo of the Weak

From a small-town weekly Texas newspaper. It puts a damper on "give and ye shall receive," and will be duly deposited in our "gee, thanks . . ." file.

> For his efforts to inoculate all the residents before the illness spread further, Dr. Ainsworth was given a plague by our grateful mayor.

Typo of the Weak

From a Louisiana town's weekly newspaper. It will be duly deposited in our "first things first; siblings, second" file.

> Police Chief [Jones] initially wanted to ensure that his brothel was out of harm's way.

Typo of the Weak

From an L.A. realtor's E-mail pitch to an upper-crust, East Coast, about-to-be-transferred client. It brings new meaning to the term "filthy rich."

> In the Los Angeles area, Brentwood is recognized as one of the most effluent communities in the country.

Chapter Eight

Those Hallowed Halls

Can anyone tell me why it's called higher education? Higher than what? Is K–12 lower education? Just wondering. Just as I wonder why the folks in our neighborhood spend tons of money for these purebred dogs and then fence them in runs in the backyard or put in invisible fencing so they don't have to bother to walk them. What is the point?

A woman in Wisconsin called the English department of her local college with a question about the rule for "a" or "an" before a word beginning with a vowel. They told her to call the Grammar Hotline. Now I ask you what depths have we sunk to when the folks in a college English department don't know this one? I guess 'twas ever thus. The English department at the University of Pittsburgh often referred grammar questions to us in Linguistics. Meanwhile, see more on the Wisconsin question below.

When I finished college in the long-lost 1960s, many of my female colleagues had achieved the Mrs. degree they'd sought from the beginning, but were fully equipped with skills to be teachers or nurses or to move into the other careers then open to women. When our daughter graduates in the year 2000, she and her colleagues, who seem relatively uninterested in marriage and family, will need advanced degrees to be qualified to do much of anything. Do I sound struck by this irony? Maybe, just a tad. We have friends whose daughter finally finished graduate school and found a pretty good teaching job. You guessed it—the wedding is in October.

Well, I guess I've dithered long enough, time to look at how I can help the college crowd.

A college student wondered if he was unique in thinking that the function of written or spoken language is to communicate, and therefore it doesn't matter whether one has the comma in the right place or says may/can or whatever, so long as the person he is dealing with knows what he's going on about. Unfortunately he is not unique; there are many people who feel exactly as he does, and they increase each year that the schools insist on "feel-good, do-your-own-thing" policies about correctness in language. But, if the monthly increase in visits to my Web site and on my 800 phone bill is any indication, there is a growing sense that sloppiness in language use is accompanied by sloppiness in thought and other areas of endeavor.

THE PAPER CHASE

For a thesis, a student needed to know what form the verb "provide" should be in this sentence: "The type of writing demands that the author *provide/s* sufficient details." Since a thesis is usually a pretty formal document requiring a formal style, the verb following "that" needs to be in the subjunctive form (without an "s"). This occurs when the verb in the main sentence contains an expression of recommendation, resolution, demand, and so forth. Therefore, "The type of writing demands that the author provide sufficient details." Note that this is true in formal speaking and especially in written styles; it is generally not observed in less formal styles because it seems stilted.

How are the quotation marks handled in a college paper if there is a long quotation consisting of several paragraphs? First of all, my advice is to try to avoid this technique if it's merely for filler. Professors will spot gratuitous long quotations a mile away. That said, quotation marks appear at the beginning of each paragraph, but at the end of the last paragraph only.

A student in charge of editing a program needed to know how to punctuate titles of individual dances performed by university students at a senior recital. She guessed quotation marks and she was right. Just to complete the answer: books, names of journals, newspapers, and plays are underlined or italicized. (It doesn't matter which, but many schools have a style sheet they want students to follow; so it's good to know what that is *before* starting to write the paper.) Place in quotation marks titles of articles from journals, book chapters, poems, song titles, and magazine articles.

If there is material in parentheses at the end of a sentence, a student wanted to know, does the final punctuation go inside or out of the closing parenthesis? It depends on the relationship of the material to the rest of the sentence. If the whole sentence is parenthetical, the end punctuation goes inside. *(This sentence is an example.)* If the parenthetical material is at the end of an otherwise normal sentence, it goes outside. *The man was a wealthy retiree with several homes (according to his story).*

LET'S GO SURFING NOW

A West Virginia University student (usually they don't tell me the school) had a question. He had an assignment for a technical writing class given through E-mail and Internet. (I don't know if that meant he never met with a real person. I certainly hope not.) He was given an incorrect sentence and was told to find a Web site to help him correct the error. When he came upon my site he thought I could help. Here is the sentence: "Looking at several search engines, they seem to be complicated to use." He was supposed to correct the statement, provide a description of the error, and send the response to the professor. I told him it was a dangling participle. Who is doing the "looking"? They? Think about "Smothered in ketchup, I ate the juicy hamburger" or "I gazed lovingly into her eyes lying on a grassy knoll." I hope he fleshed out my response a little before he sent it in. I have a pretty strict rule against doing homework without teacher authorization, but this guy seemed very sincere and appealed to my soft spot.

I was impressed by a solicitous husband who wanted to know where his wife, a college returnee, could find information on-line about proper methods of footnoting her book reports. I don't know where to go on-line, but there is a little book I consider absolutely necessary: *The Little, Brown Essential Handbook for Writers* by Jane Aaron. You can get it from on-line bookstores if there is not a source near you.

A student designing a Web page for a Utah college club was caught between a grammatical rock and a geographical hard place. She wanted to know why "an Utah college student" sounds awkward when obviously the word written after "a" begins with a vowel. It sounds as if it should be written "a Utah college student." She and her classmates tried to develop a grammar rule that says that descriptive words (adjectives) are ignored. While I applaud their initiative, they are wrong. We say "an honorable college student." What's relevant is not that the letter is a vowel or consonant, but the beginning *sound* of the word, in this case *y*. If the *u* is pronounced like a vowel, then we'd use "an" as in "an underhanded deal." The same rule applies to *o*—"a one-horse town," "an onerous task."

To recap, "a" is used before consonant sounds and "an" before vowel sounds without regard for whether the letter is considered a vowel or a consonant. The major problems are words starting with *h* (a consonant letter), and *u* and *o* (vowel letters). *H* is silent at the beginning of a very few words: hour, honest. When it is silent, "an" precedes: an hour; an honest man. When it is not silent, "a" precedes: a history book, a historical figure. (Why people use "an" in the last example mystifies me, except that the *h* might be silent in British English. It is *not* silent in American English.)

THE NAKED AND THE LED

I'm not sure why, but Canadians are overrepresented in my queries from academics. Maybe it has something to do with the longer winter in Canada, or maybe because it's a bilingual country. Anyway, a Canadian professor wondered about the use of the naked "this." "This means that he is being effective. There is nothing objectionable to this." He is seeing more and more of this (kind of thing) in his students' papers. It is sometimes opaque, though one can usually figure out the intended referent; but it strikes him as lazy. I hadn't noticed this phenomenon, but I agree that not much thought has been exerted to connect the ideas with more complex sentence

---

WORRISOME WORD

ETHOS (Note: *th* as in thirsty. EE-thus, EE-those, ETH-us, ETH-ose) n. The underlying character, beliefs, or assumptions of a culture or group of people. *The ethos of the Puritans included strict religious observance, hard work and frugality, and the denial of frivolous pleasure and entertainment.*

structure. I guess we'll have to scrutinize *this* book and root *these* out. Oops, is that a naked "these"?

Another Canadian professor has had a long-standing argument with an American professor of English who claims that someone cannot be "lead," they must be "led." He was looking for the correct spelling of the past tense action "to lead someone by the hand." "I *lead/led* him away from the scene." Only "led" is correct in American English as the past tense of "to lead." I have seen it erroneously spelled "lead" because the metal or the black stuff in a pencil (lead) is pronounced the same as the past tense of the verb.

Yet another Canadian wanted to know if there is a term (from linguistics, perhaps?) for the way that people use the word *like* as in *It was . . . like . . . cold.* I think "inarticulate stutter" pretty well covers it as a term, though hardly linguistic in origin. He thought it interesting that this usage is confined to speech. He had never seen it in writing, except when someone is quoting someone else. We can thank our lucky Canadian and American stars for that.

FACULTY FOLLY

I've been asked to settle bets, patch up marital discords, and referee office debates but when a college teacher asked me to be an expert witness, even I was nonplussed. She described a situation in which a student had signed her name and entered a grade on an official withdrawal form from a course. The student asserted that the form read "instructor's approval" above the line for the instructor's name, not "instructor's signature," and thus the student was supposed to enter only the instructor's name on the line. The college teacher wrote me, "I assert that 'approval' denotes 'to confirm authoritatively' and that 'instructor's' acting as possessive of 'approval' means that it is the instructor's approval that is required and attested to via that person's signature. ('Instructor' alone might be vague but 'approval' in connection with that suggests to me that the instructor needs to be involved in the process of dropping a course.) As for the grade, I assert that instructors are the only ones with authority to assign grades and thus are the ones to fill the grade in the slot. The student asserts that he can fill in his own grade on the basis of his understanding of how he is doing in a course. The grammatical-linguistic issue here has to do with the possessive of 'instructor' as it relates to 'approval' and the context of the phrase 'instructor's approval.' "

Phew. Pardon me while I catch my breath here.

The linguistic hairsplitting is totally irrelevant. I think the underlying issue is nothing less than forgery. There has to be a line in the faculty handbook that only instructors can sign the forms and anything else is forgery. The student should be expelled at once and left to his own grammatical mishaps.

College instructors aren't the only academic employees who can be grammatically challenged. The college president's secretary was editing a report and asked if a sentence could begin with "and" or "but." My attitude is that there is nothing wrong with doing this once in a while to provide variety of sentence structure. But be judicious. And think about it carefully. And then decide for yourself. But remember what I said. And then mentally rewrite this paragraph.

The P.R. office wants a new brochure touting "the myriad new choices of majors." They wonder if this use of "myriad" is correct. Yes, it is. But they should avoid "a myriad of" and any use of the plural form.

✳**Goofy Goof:** The boss sent a memo with this sentence: Do to lack of funds, we will no longer be able . . .

CALLING ALL ALUMN

A woman who ran a Web site for her alumni association wanted to know how to refer to a generic individual who is a member of a mixed gender group. In writing a solicitation, she wanted to be both grammatically and *politically* correct! She was considering the following construction: "Any ALUMN _____ may submit suggestions, but must be approved by a majority of the affected alumni." She felt that substituting another word such as *person* or *graduate* would be taking the easy way out and therefore not an option. I'm not sure why substitution isn't an option, but it's the only correct solution to her dilemma.

Alumn is not a word, nor is *alum* as in "Because you're a Penn State alum . . ." It is short for alumnus, and so should be avoided in all but the least formal situations. By the way, "alumnus" is the singular of "alumni," not the other way around. To be even more specific: alumnus is singular masculine; alumni, plural masculine; alumna, singular feminine; alumnae, plural feminine. The people to whom these words apply *know* which one is right; if you use the wrong one, you expose yourself as an ignoramus. Or ignorama, as the case may be. (It's like yelling Bravo! at the opera. Cognoscenti yell Brava! at the soprano, Bravo! at the tenor, and Bravi! at the chorus.)

A college treasury official wanted to know if the following sentence had the commas in the correct places: "Because the endowment is not adequate, we rely, more than many of our peer institutions, on tuition income to fund student aid." Bravo! Indeed they are.

One school's alumni association board wondered if alumni association board should be capitalized in the following sentence. "Our Alumni Association Board will be holding its evaluation in

June." If the words are the official name of the organization, then yes. Also, should university be capitalized on second reference if it's used alone? On first reference it would be "Spalding University students have their final exams next week." On second reference, "The university will be closed next week for final exams." When these words are used in a general sense they are in lowercase: universities, professors, the humanities. When there is a specific reference, they are capitalized: the University of Illinois, Professors Doe and Wade, the Department of Linguistics.

Whether "the" in a school's name is capitalized is highly idiosyncratic. We have The Ohio State University, but the University of Pittsburgh.

TRAINING THE TRAINERS: TEACHERS

There's been a lot of grumbling about the competence of teachers lately; maybe we should scrutinize the schools supposedly training them.

In "Polishing the Apple," I told you what I think should happen vis-à-vis teaching grammar in the public school. It goes without saying that teachers must be taught how to carry out such a program. The design of a specific program is beyond the scope of this book—not that I couldn't do it, mind you—but various people have called regarding such courses at college, so I feel compelled to address them.

A teacher from a college in the Midwest had read the article where I held forth on the horrors of diagraming. She taught an advanced grammar class, including how to teach diagraming, for prospective teachers and wondered what I felt about the practice at that level. I asked her my standard question: "Why are you doing it?" There was a long pause, and she finally said because it was in the textbook. In my own teaching career, once I got over following the text, the first question I asked myself in planning each lesson was, "What do I want the students to learn from this and why do they need to know it?" If I didn't have a good answer, I abandoned the topic. "Because it's in the text" never cut the mustard. (In case you thought I didn't know where "cut the mustard" came from . . . it's a cowboy term from the late 1800s, meaning "the real McCoy," absolutely the real thing. The meaning has changed over the years to mean something like "to be successful." You'll have to wait for another tome to find out about McCoy.)

I wasn't going to get into a lengthy discussion of her teaching philosophy, so I asked her how the students felt about it. She said half liked it and the others didn't like it at all. I remarked that that was a pretty high percentage of negatives. I suggested that she give the students model sentences and get them to write new ones with identical structures. That way she could tell if they understood the structure and what they didn't understand if they went wrong, which seems a lot more meaningful than a mechanical diagraming exercise. She thought this was worth a try. I asked her to call back and tell me how it worked, but so far she hasn't.

I was able to test my own pedagogy shortly thereafter with another nontraditional student who was taking a course in communications that turned out to be Grammar 101. She had failed a quiz because she couldn't identify the parts of speech in sentences such as: "The President is ready to throw his support to whomever the party nominates." Yet when I asked, she was able to identify the

---

SANCTIMONIOUS (sank-tih-MO-nee-us) adj. Hypocritical show of religious devotion, with pretended piety; self-righteous. *The mother of the worst bully in school was making sanctimonious comments about the bad behavior of kids today.*

verbs and then the subjects and finally the objects of this very complex sentence. In five minutes we had dissected the sentence as completely as if it had been diagramed. Furthermore, she seemed confident to ask herself such questions in the future.

Trust Californians to be ahead of every educational curve, whether or not they are on the right road. According to an article in the *San Francisco Chronicle*, they're switching from the "whole language" method of teaching reading to "phonics." It's half of what I described as a reasonable approach in the "Polishing the Apple" chapter. The problem is that the teachers are virtually going to have to become linguistics specialists in order to teach the curriculum, a sure-fire way to deep-six the program. I was taught by the phonics method as I have pointed out elsewhere, and I'm fairly sure my first-grade teacher didn't know the meaning of "phoneme—an abstract concept manifested in actual speech as a phonetic variant, such as the allophones of a phoneme." California educators switched to "whole language" in 1987, and I predict they'll be switching to something else by 2007. These educators should ask themselves the question I put to myself: What do the teachers need to know and why do they need to know it?

A nontraditional (read: older than usual) student at a local teacher preparation institute is taking a class in how to teach language arts. He asked if I could help him with a "linear" approach to teaching grammar. The caller had looked at the examples the professor had put on his Web page (there's that Internet cropping up again) and set about designing an exercise to teach vocabulary to young students. The professor said he hadn't done it right, but didn't provide any feedback about what he'd done wrong. I said that it didn't seem very helpful considering what he was paying out in tuition. The caller thought that his professor was just mirroring the way it would be when a teacher was in the classroom. There wouldn't be anyone to help then. Now, what kind of message is that to send? Is that how this new teacher is to teach his students?

Throw some exercises on the board and tell the children, "You figure it out"?

With teachers like that, no wonder I wind up receiving the kind of correspondence from college students given in the section below.

INQUIRING MINDS

A student complained that her instructor had circled every instance of "alot" in her compositions. I should hope so; the proper spelling is two words, "a lot." You wouldn't put "a little" together, would you? (See front cover of this book for much further ado on this subject.)

An undergraduate kept getting "any way" and "anyway" mixed up. The two-word phrase is an adjective plus noun: "Is there any way you can get this paper in today?" The single word is an adverb: "It's raining, but we're going to hold the rally anyway."

A student's law professor was always talking about people being "disinterested" or "uninterested" but the student couldn't get the difference. A "disinterested" judge is neutral with nothing to gain or lose whatever the outcome. An "uninterested" judge has no interest whatever and might fall asleep if the proceedings get slow.

In an article quoting a college professor, no less, I found this

WORRISOME WORD

EQUANIMITY (ee-kwuh-NIHM-ih-tee) n. Calmness, mental or emotional composure under stressful conditions. *She never lost her equanimity; even in the ambulance on the way to the emergency room, she remained calm and assured us that everything would be fine.*

spectacular grammar goof: "Jay Powell, professor of special education, said, 'Myself and some others are working on a bill of particulars for a vote of no confidence.' " Myself is working . . . ??? I don't think so.

The mother of an English major feels she may have been short-changed in her investment in higher education. Her college graduate daughter insists that "It is I" is incorrect, and that it should be "It is me." Mom asked whether the rules had changed about predicate nominative, or whether she should send her daughter back for a master's degree? The rules have not changed, but "It is I" is deemed very formal albeit correct. People who want to avoid the formality find different ways of identifying themselves in response to the question "Is this Mary?" Some say "Speaking," "Yes," "'Tis I," or "This is Mary." Maybe the woman should ask the college for a refund.

When a University of Pittsburgh sophomore, who was doing a project that focused on the debate over the importance of understanding grammar rules and how to teach these rules, wanted input, my trusty on-line recreational grammar pals came to her aid.

Hogwash wrote:

There are many difficulties connected with rules. An external observer knows not when rules are being followed and when they are broken. Hence, we have the problem of "obeying rules" and "following rules." And to the participants themselves, how do we know, when they say such-and-such that they are merely acting in accordance with a rule (without their knowing it) or that they are knowingly obeying or following obediently the rule. Kant gives more value to those who know the rules and follow them.

To teach grammar is to read grammar. To teach sentence structure is to read Hemingway for the simple paratactic; Faulkner for the complex hypotactic. Read and discuss the forms of the works—skip plot, characterization, place, etc. Talk about style, sentence syntax, nouns and verbs. Describe what these writers do—and you have taught grammar-as-applied. You can't do better.

KD added:

I agree with all of the above, but we haven't touched on the question, how to teach? I think the basic names for things— noun, verb, interrogative should be taught in the early elementary grades with texts that the children like to read and that they understand. Then the language can be examined per se. "This story is told in the past, but the things the character says are in the present—Why?" This kind of instruction should be completed by the end of sixth grade at the latest. Then application of Hogwash's program would turn out some pretty literate people.

I couldn't have said it better if I tried. Actually, I did try and I have said it! (See page 22 in chapter 1.)

RÉSUMÉ REDUX

Nowhere is the need for correct grammar more essential than when one is moving from college student to citizen of the world—and writing one's first résumé. It's critically important to present a perfect job in order to land the perfect job. So without further ado (see

---

❋**Goofy Goof:** On a Maine shop: Our motto is to give our customers the lowest possible prices and workmanship.

cover again) I will tell you how to avoid some pitfalls. Some are common, while others are more idiosyncratic.

The first thing people writing résumés need to know is how to capitalize degrees properly. For example, if you received a Master's Degree of Fine Arts in Creative Writing are the words *creative writing* capitalized or do they remain lowercase? The complete title of the degree is uppercase. The subject or area of studies is lowercase. I personally have a doctorate in linguistics; my husband has a degree in mechanical engineering. My editor has a master's in journalism.

When discussing degrees, someone wondered what the proper way to refer to an associate or associate's degree would be. Bachelor's degrees and master's degrees seem to require apostrophes because they are alternatives for bachelor of art or master of science. Does this hold true for the associate degree? I opened the Associated Press style book, full of confidence that the answer would be there, but darned if it is not! Logic says that associate's degree ought to follow right along with master's and bachelor's, but grammar is so often not logical. We'll decree that it's analogous—associate's.

In a list of skills on a résumé "Proficient in Internet usage" is technically grammatically correct, although I'm not quite sure what it means. Perhaps it would be better to be specific. In what way are you proficient in Internet usage? Researching subjects on the Internet? The way it is written, it could just mean that you waste a lot of time surfing.

There is often confusion about using "make" and "makes" in résumés. In the following sentence, what would be the right verb form? "I believe that my considerable experience in the multimedia industry *make/s* me an attractive candidate." I say, look to the subject! The subject is "experience," so the verb is "makes."

One student was yearning to be a model of résumé correctness, an attitude I like to encourage. She wanted me to answer quickly because she needed to mail her cover letter and résumé *tout de suite.* (I love to throw in these little foreign phrases every now and again, just to keep my readers on their toes.) She was trying to choose between "I will be graduating in May" or "I will be graduated in May." Either "I will graduate in May" or "I will be graduating in May" would do. "I will be graduated" sounds old-fashioned for today's résumés.

Another tricky capitalization question concerns the much sought although sometimes maligned letter of recommendation. So often I see: "I am extremely pleased to give this Letter of Recommendation for Joel Berry." I would not capitalize "letter of recommendation." It makes the phrase look more important than it really is.

THE MULTICULTURAL COLLEGE, OR AROUND THE WORLD WITH THE GRAMMAR LADY

A young man, who had lived in Venezuela since the age of five, recently returned to the United States. He learned English when he

---

WORRISOME WORD

TAUTOLOGICAL (taught-uh-LODGE-ih-cull) adj. Redundant, circular. The expression "widow woman" is tautological, because all widows are also women. A tautology is a repetition of words, or giving the same information using different words. At a recent church service, the congregation was told that when it came time for the hymn we were to open the hymnals and sing the song together. My teenaged daughter turned to me and went, "Duh," which seems to be the sensible reaction to tautologies.

was about eleven, but remained in Venezuela, and Spanish is his native tongue. Now in his twenties, he wants to start college here. He reads many, many English magazines, and speaks English well. So when he took a college placement test, he was shocked to find his English vocabulary lacking. He doesn't know the meaning of words like *brood*. Since he's a bit of a hacker, he wanted names of Web sites with vocabulary tests and vocabulary builders. I told him to check the homeschool sites and those run by the different dictionaries. For those of you who still prefer off-line to on-line the reference sections of bookstores also have such texts.

A college student wanted to know why certain words are considered to be "bad." He wrote, "Is it because they have Anglo-Saxon origins, rather than Latin, Norman, or French ones? For example, 'sit' is never considered a 'bad' word, and 'defecate' is considered acceptable, but a word that sounds very similar to the one and means the same as the other is considered 'bad.' Is there a logical explanation of some sort for this?"

The clever way he phrased this question inspired me to take a shot at an answer. In the first place different cultures have different ideas of what "bad" words are. Our culture seems to find references to bodily functions particularly distasteful. Indeed, within a culture changes happen in these matters all the time. The original Anglo-Saxon words were the ones everyone knew and used, but when fashion dictated that these topics were not appropriate, the words became taboo along with the subject. However, people still needed to address the issues, medically, if not socially; so a new set of words was needed. The Latinate versions seemed unfamiliar and didn't carry the original taboo; therefore, they were acceptable. A similar change is going on today in the politically correct labels for ethnic groups, people with various handicaps, etc. It's certainly not logical but more like fashion in cultural orientation reflected by language use.

An international student challenged an American teacher on this sentence the teacher had written! "She would rather spend her time having intellectual conversations and going to lectures and classical concerts than living a life of fantasy and talking about romance and fashion like many other young women her age." The American writer thought that "having/going" were parallel in structure to "living/talking," but the international friend thought the verb "live" should be parallel to "spend." I agree that "going" is parallel with "having." The meaning changes if you make it "spend." Sometimes people who know the technicalities of grammar lose sight of the meaning. Can't see the sentence for the words syndrome?

Finally, a friend who studies anthropology and linguistics told a student that the word *healthy* is grammatically incorrect and that the correct adjective form is "healthful." We have become accustomed to "healthy" even though it is incorrect. I think the battle for "healthful" may be lost. I am aware that living languages change even if I like to preserve the distinction among words as long as possible. And that I love to have the last word!

Grammar Points

punctuation of a dance
punctuating a long quotation
subjunctive verb
parentheses at the end of a sentence
dangling participles
a/an before letters
bibliographic reference

✳**Goofy Goof:** Here are a couple of food goofs: Barely Soup and Eye-round Steak with Peepers.

spelling lead/led
naked "this"
"like" stutter
and/but at beginning of sentence
myriad
commas
capitalizing degrees
alumni
associate's degree
capitalization of organization names
teacher training
diagraming—advanced level
phonics to teach reading
a lot
understanding sentence structure
imply/infer
résumés
subject-verb agreement
disinterested/uninterested
vocabulary learning
reflexive pronoun
it is I/me
taboo words
healthy/healthful
parallel structure

MARY'S BEE

Here's a suffering suffix quiz. The challenge is to add the suffix and end up with a correctly spelled new word!

1. false + ify

2. nice + ly

3. rude + ness

4. police + ing

5. use + able

6. use + less

7. courage + ous

8. landscape + ing

9. nine + ty

10. sore + ly

THE QUIZZICAL I

Many people have trouble with imply and infer. The verbs are similar in meaning because they have to do with communications that are not stated directly, messages that are "read between the lines." The person who sends such a message implies it; the person who receives it infers it. *Tip:* You should be able to substitute "suggest" for "imply" and "understand" for "infer" without changing the meaning of the sentence. For example: *I inferred (understood) from the tone of her voice that she was not pleased. He implied (suggested) that he would be sending the money soon.* I'm sure you now grasp the difference, but to reinforce your knowledge, take this quiz.

1. We implied/inferred from his remarks that he was a friend of the family.

2. She implied/inferred that she could have us fired.

3. The police implied/inferred from the sequence of events how the accident had happened.

4. Did she imply/infer their body language correctly?

5. Did he mean to imply/infer that I was lying?

6. I implied/inferred from the look on her face that she was very angry.

7. They implied/inferred that they were going to bid on the house themselves.

8. Did you imply/infer the same message as I got from his speech?

Typo of the Weak

From a rural Tennessee paper's review of a local summer comedy that, apparently, folks were dying to see. Tsk, tsk. A wandering, gremlinesque *s* in a late-night deadline can bring such sorrow to laughter.

The slaughter continued, and soon they were all rolling in the aisles.

Typo of the Weak

From a New Jersey fire marshal's notification to a building manager, it will be duly deposited in our "speedy appraisals" file.

We need to ensure that the building can be evaluated in under two minutes.

Typo of the Weak

From the brochure of a Wisconsin builder, who no doubt places a grandma-stitched "Homely Sweet Homely" wall hanging in every new house.

[Buildemthicker] homes have been insulted to withstand those fierce winter blasts.

Typo of the Weak

From an informant in rural Georgia who swears she saw this Halloween special in a mom-n-pop grocery store window. Seems like a no-win situation.

Sale! Trick or Threat Candies Half Price!

Chapter Nine

The Human Condition—In God We Trust

So there I was trying to find a way into this chapter on grammar in the realm of medicine and religion, when I got an answer to my prayers in the form of a letter from a Canadian. His insurance company had denied a claim he had filed after an accident a few years ago. He now has a cyst on a body part that shall remain unnamed for purposes of delicacy. He wanted the Grammar Lady to look at his claim and interpret a paragraph, which supposedly supports his suit. For this assistance he included two Canadian dollars, called Loonies. God does provide, in more ways than one. Unfortunately I couldn't help him; I have an unbreakable rule not to advise in legal matters.

CALLING THE DOCTOR

Let's start with how to address medical professionals. In a letter to two physicians who are married to each other, the letter is addressed to Drs. John and Mary Doe. The salutation would be Dear

Drs. Doe. As is normal in written communication, the man's name goes first. However if the woman holds a title and the man doesn't her name goes first: Dr. Mary and Mr. John Doe. The salutation then is Dear Dr. and Mr. Doe. My, that does sound odd, I must admit.

This makes me wonder about the word *woman* used as an adjective as in *women doctors* rather than *female doctors*. I'm not sure when it became popular, but I surely would like it to disappear, along with *male nurse*. Don't misunderstand, *male nurse* and *female doctor* are grammatically correct. But it seems to me that nurses and doctors of both genders (to use Judge Ruth Bader Ginsburg's term) have the same training for their jobs, so why do we need the qualification?

Some physicians can really make us confused by using a name, a numeral, and a professional title, e.g., John Doe III M.D. How do we punctuate that? The numeral is essential to the man's identity, so it is not set off by a comma. The professional title is not essential presumably, although I'm sure if you were about to undergo, say, brain surgery, you would beg to differ. Anyway, the correct punctuation is John Doe III, M.D.

Conversely, what if your surgeon operates on the wrong part of you? For improper behavior a priest is defrocked, a lawyer is disbarred. Is there a similar word for taking away a doctor's license? Maybe dis/decaduceus? There is a term in British English: When a medical doctor does something wrong, he or she is "struck off the rolls" and is no longer allowed to practice. There's a fascinating

---

WORRISOME WORD

SAGACIOUS (suh-GAY-shus) adj. Wise, shrewd, able to use information to make good decisions. A related noun is sage: a wise person is sometimes called a sage. *The move from Pennsylvania to New Mexico proved sagacious; the next five winters in Pennsylvania got worse and worse.*

expression: "to practice" medicine or law. Teachers do "practice teaching" and then become teachers, but doctors and attorneys "practice" throughout their careers. I'm sure I could make something of that, but I've got to finish the rest of this book on deadline.

OFFICE VISITS

Not only does grammar matter, it can be a matter of life and death!

Say you're at the doctor's office and he is giving you the results of some blood tests. You're not quite sure what he means. Do you use the word *imply* or *infer?* If you are referring to what the doctor has said, it's "Do you mean to imply that the test is positive?" If you are referring to what you think you heard, it's "Am I to infer that it is negative?" The sPeaker imPlies and the listenER infERs. We certainly want to understand the good doctor, do we not?

A non-life-threatening but oh so annoying point is that too many nurses in too many doctors' offices say, "Put on the gown and lay down on the table." A nurse has to say this so many times a day, why can't she get it right? It's lie, not lay, but you knew that by now, didn't you? Some people still think that the distinction between lay and lie is between living things and nonliving things. Sillies. "Lay" is to put or place something: lay the baby down. "Lie" is to recline: the patient is lying on the table. If in doubt, use the old "A chicken lays eggs" test. You wouldn't want to leave eggs in the doctor's office, after all.

Meanwhile, a gynecologist from New York (his accent gave him away) called to tell me how much of a picky person he is about grammar. Two English teachers in a row whom he had told to "lay down" in the examination room had corrected him to say "lie down." He thought it was very funny how two patients in a row could be wrong. When I told him they were right and he was wrong, he was truly flabbergasted. I wouldn't be a bit surprised to hear he's changed careers.

JUST A HYPHEN OR NOT MAKES THE MEDICINE GO DOWN

The language of medicine is a rich area for the Grammar Lady to mine. Is it a HMO or an HMO? A X-ray technician or an X-ray technician? Listen to the sound at the beginning of the letter to figure these out. They both begin with a vowel sound, so "an" is correct in both cases.

Why do we still spell X-ray with a hyphen? Usually, the hyphen disappears when a word becomes established in the language. If the hyphen were to disappear from this word, we would be left with xray, which is not easily pronounced by speakers of English. Hyphens are also left in words that would be confusing without them: co-op and co-ed, for example. And if those are not exceptions enough, hyphens are also required before proper nouns: pro-Arab. (No angry letters please, it's just an example off the top of my head.)

Getting back to articles and technicians, young colleagues of a technician doing lab reports insist that "paucity" does not require the article "a" before it. They claim "There is paucity of blood" is correct. The report should read "There is a paucity of blood." I know of only one singular noun that does not require an article (a, an, the), and it's not paucity. It's "anathema" and no, I don't know why it doesn't. Luckily, a colleague of mine thinks she might know. The term originally implied a condition imposed by the church, a formal ecclesiastical curse involving excommunication. Now it means something loathed: "Politics are anathema at some people's dinner table." The same reasoning would dictate why we do not say "an arthritis" or "a cancer." Although in French it is *Il a un cancer de la peau* or "He has a cancer of the skin." Public service announcement: Please do remember to wear lots of sunscreen. Otherwise you risk not only cancer but premature aging.

"Who ages better, men or women?" I would not hazard a guess, but I do know I'm not crazy about the punctuation of this sentence. I think a dash or another question mark would be better. The real fuss is about using a singular verb with a plural answer. The word "who" as a question and subject always takes a singular verb because the person asking doesn't know what the answer will be. (Exactly as we do not know whether men or women age better.) "Who is at the door? John and Mary." Even if I know there are two people at the door, the question is "Who is at the door?" In a rhetorical question the rule still stands.

Did you know that more than germs can make us sick? (That's a rhetorical question, if ever there was one.) The extremely widespread misuse of nauseated and nauseous is downright sickening. "Nauseated" is a description of how one feels. "Nauseous" is whatever is causing one to feel nauseated. I think if you can't remember this distinction, you should avoid the issue and stick to sickening and sickened.

One poor patient complained to his doctor of pains in his wrists. He wondered if he had hurt his muscles and whether he should try strengthening them. The doctor replied that the term "strengthening of wrist muscles" was an oxymoron because the wrist has no muscles. The patient didn't think this was an oxymoron. Perhaps a misstatement, but not a contradiction of terms such as "hot ice" or "angelic fiend." Two entities need to be juxtaposed to create an oxymoron. I guess to this physician there were two distinct things, although my layman's eyes don't see them. Oxymorons, like beauty, seem to be in the eye of the beholder. My favorite oxymoron is "Forever Wild Development Corporation."

Meanwhile, maybe the wrist sufferer should try holistic medicine.

I've often wondered why holistic is not spelled with a "w," if it's concerned with the "whole" person. The term is attributed to South African philosopher J. C. Smuts, who stated that (contrary to mathematical principles) whole entities are greater than or different from the sum of their parts. That doesn't explain why it was spelled without the "w." Later writers relate the word to "holy" or "healing."

Other words can be deceptive little devils. Take *triage:* you might think its root is "three" or "tri," even if you had no idea what it meant. That would be utterly logical because in triage, the wounded are divided into three groups.

1. Those who will live even though they do not receive immediate treatment are put aside to be treated later.
2. Those who will die even with immediate treatment are put aside to be treated later.
3. Those who may live with immediate treatment, but will die without it, are treated first.

We may be uncomfortable considering group number two, but it is with group number three that the medical teams can make a difference in survival, and that is where they put their first effort. This may be what happens in triage, but the base word of triage is *trier,* French for "sort." The prefix "tri" in English would be applied mistakenly to the French word that has nothing to do with three.

WORRISOME WORD

SANGUINE (SANG-gwin) adj. Confident, cheerfully hopeful. *The team was sanguine about its chances to make the playoffs, even though they had a pretty dismal season record. "We always play better at the end of the season," said the captain.* (Note: The related word *sanguinary*, also an adjective, has a seemingly opposite meaning. Sanguinary means bloodthirsty, cruel.

To be precise within a professional field, jargon is often necessary. I don't begrudge anyone his professional lingo in house. What I dislike is the use of new terms for old concepts in an attempt to make nonprofessionals think something new is afoot. The word *behavior* is a recent example. The total of a person's actions constitutes his behavior; however, psychologists and social workers love to say "behaviors." Maybe they think they can charge more to treat behaviors instead of behavior.

This winter I hear radio commentators talking about "incidences of this or that disease." There seems to be a new confusion between the words *incident* and *incidence*. The word *incident* means occurrence and can be used in the plural: *There have been many incidents of flu-related deaths this winter*. The word *incidence* means the rate or range of occurrence of something and is not normally used as a plural: *The incidence of adult-onset asthma has increased dramatically over the last decade*.

YOU SAY FLUSHES, I FEEL FLASHES

It's far easier for the Grammar Lady to explain a rare condition than it is for the doctor to diagnose it. Take macropsia (muh-KROP-see-uh), a visual disorder that makes objects appear larger than their actual size. Micropsia is the opposite; objects appear smaller than their actual size. I rest my case.

A more mundane condition affects half the population upon reaching a certain age. If you experience this female complaint, do you experience hot flashes or flushes? I have read both used interchangeably, but more often see "flashes." No matter what you call it, it's a darn nuisance.

I think we can all agree that chicken pox is a single disease. Why then do Americans talk about chicken pox as "they" and not "it"?

Apparently in England, people are more consistent. It may be that people here confuse the name of the disease with the pock marks left as the scabs are removed. Chicken pox is heard more often than it is written by most people. The word *pocks* is more common than *pox,* so this might be a form of folk etymology. Or not. I do know the scar on my nose garnered in a fight with my older brother is still visible. Ahh, to be young again.

When I *was* younger, people seemed to die "of" a disease. "She died of pneumonia," for example. Nowadays, all we hear is "die from." I'm still alive and well enough to explain that according to one usage guide, "It is equally correct to speak of dying 'of' or 'from' causes: 'to die of/from thirst.' "

How about the correct form of "heartburn"? Is it "the heartburn"? It depends on the context. Heartburn, like many conditions, such as laryngitis or athlete's foot, is referred to without the article when speaking generally. "I get heartburn when I eat certain foods." It is used with the article when referring to a special case. "The heart-burn from dinner last night was especially bad."

I wish you good physical health; may your grammatical condition improve with time. Now I will make a graceful transition to matters of the spirit. Let's see . . . many of us consider doctors almost godlike.

IN GOD WE TRUST

When I first started operating the hotline in Pittsburgh the calls were sometimes few and far between. I admit there are times when I am quite nostalgic for those days. Our daughter, Mary Beth, then ten years old, loved answering the phone; so when it rang on a Sunday morning, she grabbed it. "Mom," she called, "how do you spell 'triumphant'?" She repeated the spelling to the caller, a man, and we speculated about who would need the spelling of this word on a Sunday morning other than someone putting the finishing touches on a sermon. Even God's servants need help.

There are frequent complaints about preachers who use bad grammar. Maybe their minds are on a higher plane, but that is no excuse for asking "God's blessing on we the people" and "Thank you for the wonderful gift you gave my wife and I" and "Jesus died for you and I." If your religious leader preaches this way, I recommend writing a message on the church bulletin and slipping it to him or her on the way out. This is probably a good place to mention that frequent grammar errors in the sermon do offend parishioners and often cause them to nod off or at least stop listening. Perhaps if you have a preacher in mind, you could buy him/her a copy of this book and circle this paragraph. Not too subtle, but it might work.

A conscientious minister's secretary was flummoxed when her boss presented a letter for her to type that included this sentence: "We appreciate you visiting with us last Sunday." The secretary wanted to change it to read "We appreciate your visiting with us last Sunday."

How about it? Which one is right? The secretary, of course. "Your visiting" is correct because the possessive pronoun is used before a verb ending in *ing* (a gerund). Teachers say "use possessive before a gerund," but did you ever hear why? Well, here's the deal. A gerund is a noun made from a verb—*visit* (n) + *ing*. Let's try a regular noun in the same space, say "attention." "We appreciate you/your attention." Now it's clear that it's "your." Just another tip for your grammar toolbox.

At this exact point in the manuscript preparation someone called to ask if the third person singular is correct in the phrase from Romans 6:23 "The wages of sin is death." He thought it should be "are." I told him to consider it poetic license. Also, here is one clearcut case of substance being a tad more important than form. Oh no, does that make me a Grammar Heretic? No matter. It will be a very cold day when the Grammar Lady attempts to rewrite the Bible.

Others have no such qualms. It seems there is a new translation of the Bible for children in which "ark" is changed to "big boat" and "plowshares" is replaced by "garden tools." However, the church leaders objected to having Mary lay Jesus "in a feed box." When someone pointed out that the carol "Away in a Feed Box" might sound strange, "manger" was reinstated.

God truly does work in mysterious ways. I get timely questions from a person wanting to correct the Bible, and then, while editing this part of the chapter, I get a call from a kindred spirit in Chicago. She's a Catholic nun (is there any other kind of nun?) who has managed to get the phone numbers of the Chicago TV newsrooms. When she hears a grammar error, she calls to tell them. She reports that they are pretty good at receiving the criticism. She times her calls for the end of the newscast so that the offending anchor is in the office getting his coat before leaving for the day, clever nun that she is. We should make a handbook for the Grammar Guerrillas and let her be the editor.

CALLING ON THE CLERGY

Make no mistake; there is plenty of hierarchy in the church. It's especially evident in clerical titles. Quick, what do you call the Pope? Either "Your Holiness" or "Most Holy Father" is correct. Or, if you want to address a letter to a cardinal in the Catholic church, would you know how? His Eminence plus first name plus Cardinal

✳ Goofy Goof: From a menu: Home Made Soup with Leaks from Our Garden.

plus last name. His Eminence Joe Cardinal DiMona. The salutation is Your Eminence.

And how do you address a letter to a minister who also has a doctorate? If it is social correspondence, the titles are not necessary. However, assuming you want to include them all: The Reverend Dr. John Doe. (See, I told you there was a logic behind combining medicine and religion in one chapter.)

If you want to identify someone as a minister in a list of names, put the title "The Reverend" before a first and last name. Example: The Reverend Charles Doakes or The Reverend Ann Stiles. Notice that "The" is capitalized.

It is incorrect to use the title with only the last name (The Reverend Stiles) or to use Reverend with the last name, even in the salutation of a letter (Dear Reverend Doakes). The salutation should be Dear Ms./Dr. Stiles or Dear Mr./Dr. Doakes. Ms. as a title originally had no period because it is not an abbreviation, like Harry S Truman. I think most business offices use a period, now. Ah, usage.

Looking over these questions makes me wonder if only Christian folk have trouble in this area. I don't remember once being asked how to address a rabbi. Another item for my To Do list when this tome is finished.

LET US PREY

I've collected some doozies in the realm of religious word confusion. Here's a sampler:

Once someone requested a grammatical analysis of "Let us pray," which I gladly supplied. ("You" is the understood subject, "let" is the verb, "us" is the direct object, and "pray" is the bare infinitive.) I wonder why they wanted to know? I wonder even more how I answered this query and never noticed the erroneous spelling in the question until now! The Grammar Lady is only human.

"Our pastor is leaving the Church this Sunday, and the congregation wants to give him a little momentum." The editors of the church bulletin in which this sentence appeared *might* have meant he needed a kick in the you-know-where to leave town, but let's hope they meant a memento.

At a ceremony in the National Cathedral, an elderly woman buttonholed an usher and commanded, "Be sure you get me a seat up front, young man. I understand they've always had trouble with the agnostics in this place." I think the devout woman meant acoustics, but I'll never be absolutely certain.

In the bulletin, the hymn "When Morning Gilds the Sky" was printed as "guilds." This is what happens when one of a pair of homophones is forgotten, and people don't really think about what they are writing. "Guild"—an organization of people with mutual interests (the Weavers' Guild)—is only used as a noun, whereas the word in the sentence clearly is a verb. "Gild" is related to "gilt" and "gold," but this meaning seems to have been misplaced in this case.

A wedding announcement says of the groom: "He served with the United States Army in Vietnam and is a sextant at the church." Many churches have sextons to help out with the chores of the church; this might be the first church ever to employ someone as a navigational instrument.

Among classic spoonerisms were those that occurred when a lady sat down in the wrong chew in the perch. Mr. Spooner is reputed to have said, "Pardon me, Madam, but you are occupewing the wrong pie. May I sew you to another sheet?"

A song lyric I saw recently had a line, "Throw off the yolk of oppression." Do you suppose it should have been yoke?

IN THE BEGINNING

When did the practice of capitalizing the pronoun that refers to God or Jesus Christ begin? This custom is dying out nowadays, but some people want to hold on to it. Capitalization was used to indicate importance. In German all nouns are still capitalized. In English the Christian forefathers, who were in charge of things having to do with history and records—only clergy could read and write, for the most part—used capital letters to make the holy words stand out. Some of this is speculation, but it's a pretty good guess.

Another capitalization quandary involves stating that Jesus died on "The Cross." Should The and Cross be capitalized? Would only Cross be capitalized? It used to be the custom for all words, including the articles, referring to the divine were capitalized. We are not so strict today, but if you're working in a religious setting, I would capitalize them both. Having said that I just checked in the *AP Stylebook* and the articles are not capitalized. The *Random House Dictionary* entry for the cross upon which Jesus died is "Cross." After all that qualification, there's a definitive answer.

Here is a snazzy way to remonstrate against a pet peeve: misusing the adverb "hopefully." You can use this technique when people say "hopefully it won't rain" when they mean to say "I hope it won't rain on the church picnic." Instead of trying to explain the function of an adverb such as hopefully, simply ask them what they would say if they thought or knew it wouldn't rain. "Thoughtfully (Knowfully), it won't rain?" Ridiculous! Unfortunately (and that is an example), there are a lot of adverbs that modify whole sentences and appear at the beginning of sentences; the misusers of "hopefully" are following those models. They know not what they do, so treat them with kindness.

We could all use more kindness. But do we need to raise our consciences or our consciousness about being kind to others? The word *conscious* is an adjective and it means to be aware. *I was conscious of someone standing behind me.* The word *conscience* is a noun that means the awareness of right and wrong. There's a song from *Pinocchio*, I think, "Let your conscience be your guide."

And in another instance of kindness, a church bulletin lists the names of the shutins/shut-in (people who are ill at home) whom the congregants are encouraged to visit. But should the word *shutins/shut-in* include the "s"? Or is the word *shutin/shut-in* an adjective? The 1996 unabridged dictionary I use spells it with a hyphen (*shut-in*) and lists the noun usage, so "shut-ins" it is.

There was an annoying tendency this holiday season to spell "The First Noël" as "Nowell." I asked the organist at church about it and she replied, "It is an annoying fad." Maybe it will go away by next year—that's the nature of fads.

Here is an account of a church dinner I saw in the local paper. "Out in the dinning room, the men slawed cabbage. Banks of tables were set with white dishes and floral centerpieces." When did "slaw" become a verb? Wouldn't "banks of tables" have to be piled up on each other? As far as I know "slaw" is not a verb in the standard language. And while we're at it I guess if there were a very big din, we could have dinner in the "dinning" room instead of the usual dining room.

Christianity isn't the only religion with problems. In days past, practitioners of Islam were termed Moslems. The word Muslim is currently in vogue, but is there a correct or recommended spelling? The main entry in my dictionary for the definition is Muslim. At the end of the definition, the dictionary lists: *Also, Moslem, Muslem.* The problem arises because Arabic is written without vowels and because the vowel differences that we distinguish in English be-

---

✳**Goofy Goof:** This sentence appeared on a memo to students in the English department of a local college. "All work must be typed or PC'd . . ."

tween "Mos" and "Mus" and "lim" and "lem" are not important in Arabic. The spelling change from Moslem probably occurred in the 1960s when many Black Americans followed Islam and called themselves Black Muslims. That's right, folks, she leaps from religion to radical politics in a single paragraph.

A church committee decided to tack "church" onto the end of the name, The Baptist Temple, so that it would read The Baptist Temple Church in the local phone book. The thinking was that this would differentiate the congregation's identity from the Jewish temples in the neighborhood. It's a little funny to think that the congregation needs to call itself a church twice over. Anyone who is interested enough to explore an organization with the word *Baptist* in its name would have no confusion, so I don't see what the fuss was about.

BEATIFIC EXPRESSIONS?

The Bible and Shakespeare are among the most common sources for many of the phrases people wonder about such as the "skin of my teeth." It is indeed a Biblical reference, from Job 19:20. The verse goes, "My bone cleaveth to my skin and to my flesh, And I am escaped with the skin of my teeth."

Remember the discussion of the origin of the phrase "go to hell in a handbasket"? A high school research paper on the history of burial rites turned up another possible answer. From very early times people were placed in a woven basket in a fetal position as preparation for burial. Perhaps this is the source for the "hell in a handbasket" phrase. For a more secular explanation of this phrase, see page 8 in chapter 1.

The expression "just stepped out of a bandbox" puzzled us for a while. Someone suggested it should be "banded" box—one of those fancy department store boxes that are sealed with special bands. The town where I grew up had a bandstand in the middle of the common land. The musicians who came out if it were all so dressed up that I thought it was the bandbox. But according to the *Morris Dictionary of Word Origins*, we both are wrong. The bands refer to clerical bands worn around the neck, especially by Presbyterian ministers. The bandbox was for keeping the vestments clean, starched, and crisp, which is how someone would look upon "stepping out of a bandbox."

Then there's a "shibboleth." A shibboleth (SHIH-bo-leth) is a way of speaking or mode of dress that distinguishes a particular group of people. The word itself is Hebrew, and it means "grain of wheat." It was used by the people of Gilead to identify and subsequently kill the Ephraimites who could not pronounce the sound "sh." Talk about grammar matters! The story is from the Old Testament book of Judges 12:1–6.

It was bad enough to receive this E-mail, loaded with errors: "do you think it is impossible to conceive in god, but yet not exitence. (sic)" But its rutgers.edu address made it that much worse. At any rate, I deemed this a theological question, so for once I did not feel compelled to answer.

AND ON THAT NOTE . . .

In the vestry of a New England church: "Will the last person to leave please see that the perpetual light is extinguished?"

Grammar Points

---

forms of address
    two physicians married to each other
    physician with III

minister with Ph.D.
The Reverend
a Catholic cardinal
woman doctor
holistic medicine
"defrocked" physician
imply/infer
lie/lay
paucity
X-ray with or without hyphen
nauseous/nauseated
oxymoron
triage
behavior/s
incident/incidence
flashes/flushes
macro/micropesia
(the) heartburn
conscious/conscience
hopefully
shut-ins
anathema
capitalizing deity words
Moslem
church title
"hell in a handbasket"
"skin of my teeth"
shibboleth
bandbox

MARY'S BEE

And another suffix quiz for your pleasure.

1. forget + ing

2. forget + ful

3. cancel + ed

4. prefer + ing

5. prefer + able (Listen carefully to the stress.)

6. propel + er

7. benefit + ed

8. infer + ing

9. red + est

10. interfere + ing

Typo of the Weak

From a fledgling, short-lived airline's maiden flight write-up, it makes you wonder: Was it port or starboard?

All the passengers were offered a complimentary glass of domestic wing.

Typo of the Weak

From a government contractor's security-related memo to the Treasury Department (not the White House), it will be duly deposited in our "Check the Engraved Words on Our Coins" file.

The following standard is mandated, consistent with the required level of tryst.

Typo of the Weak

From a New York City hospital patient's medical chart. The doc probably told him, "Take two axle bolts in a quart of oil and call me in the morning."

The patient has been under her physician's car for two weeks.

Typo of the Weak

An oldie, certifiably cited by several informants around the country at different times and in different publications in years past, this one is dredged up from our "For the Birds" file.

For 18 years, [Flinkets, Inc.] has provided its major clients with turkey systems.

❋**Goofy Goof:** The college is a predominately women's college.

Chapter Ten

Product Will Be Hot After Heating

As the world of commerce has grown larger, so too has its influence on our lifestyle and language, and not always for the best. Take this classic example of one little slogan destroying both language and lungs with a single blow:

Winston tastes good like a cigarette should!

When this jingle debuted in a 1950s commercial, English teachers across the land let out a collective groan. They worried less about their charges developing lung cancer than the kids forever confusing the uses of the words *as* and *like.*

The distinction between "like" and "as" has become blurred in the last few decades. Used as a conjunction to introduce a clause, which has a subject and a verb, "like" is nonstandard but more and more acceptable. "It looks just as I thought it would" is preferred to "It looks just like I thought it would." "Like" as a preposition to introduce an object is a more traditional usage. "It looks like rain."

The Winston cigarette commercials annoyed a variety of people, including rabid antismokers. Even makers of cozy, "homey" products occasionally come under fire as well as smoke. Besides adding pounds, how much harm can a pound cake do? Plenty, according to English teachers. When Sara Lee ran its ad, "Nobody doesn't like Sara Lee," grammarians across the country cursed the double negative. Those grammarians were wrong. They should have to eat humble pie instead of pound cake.

Sara Lee knows that a double negative of this type is, in fact, a positive. Stay with me for a moment, please. "Nobody doesn't like Sara Lee" translates into "There is no one who dislikes Sara Lee." This means that everyone likes the company's cakes. And that is exactly the message the Sara Lee company wanted to deliver.

Some of my colleagues boycott companies that use ungrammatical language in ads. For example, many readers become annoyed when they hear children using incorrect grammar in flashy television commercials. They feel (and I concur) that these ads send an unrealistic message: that kids who use bad grammar still will be financially successful enough to buy the products being advertised. Remember that our use of grammar marks us. The budding job seeker's chances of actually securing employment rise if he knows that it's better to say, "What a lovely office you have, Ms. Jones," and not "Ain't this cool?"

Boycott is the type of protest companies understand, and those of us concerned with good grammar can be just as effective as those animal rights activists who succeeded in getting tuna companies to stop killing dolphins.

JUSTIFICATIONS

Companies that regularly misuse adverbs in their advertising seem to specialize in misusing, not to mention overusing, the words *just*

and *only*. And incorrect use can completely change the meaning of a sentence.

Here's an example. A local pizzeria recently ran an ad stating, "We just don't deliver pizza." After the home delivery business of the restaurant fell off by about 99 percent, proprietors took a good, hard look at their ad. The rewrite, "We don't just deliver pizza," was better, but not by much. What did the restaurant mean? "We don't just deliver pizza. We make it ourselves, lovingly hand-rolling the dough" is one possibility. It also might have meant, "We don't just deliver pizza, we also deliver garlic rolls and Caesar salads and soft drinks and . . ."

The placement of the word *only* can have a similar drastic effect on the meaning of a sentence. Take a look:

- *Only* I bought my cousin a pepperoni pizza. (No one else bought it.)
- I *only* bought my cousin a pepperoni pizza. (I didn't sell it to her.)
- I bought *only* my cousin a pepperoni pizza. (I didn't buy one for anyone else.)
- I bought my *only* cousin a pepperoni pizza. (I have no other cousins.)
- I bought my cousin *only* a pepperoni pizza. (I didn't buy anything else.)
- I bought my cousin a pepperoni *only* pizza. (There wasn't anything else on it.)

COMMERCIAL GOOFS AND GAFFES

The Grammar Lady has always believed that the language of advertising tries to evoke images rather than preserve logic. The proof of this hypothesis follows:

• During the Denver versus Miami playoff game (a ho-hum 38–3 affair) an Acura ad described the car as delivering "an exhilarated performance." What can this possibly mean? The performance might *be* "exhilarating," but only a person (in this case, probably the driver) can *feel* "exhilarated."

• *Need a Reason to Buy a Jaguar Now? Here's Three.* So ran the ad in a major newspaper. One can only hope that the people who actually have the cash to buy Jaguars know the correct phrasing. Even without the cash anyone with an ounce of grammar sense knows that the subject follows "here" and "there." "Here is a Jaguar. Here are three reasons to buy one."

• Kraft foods ran an advertisement picturing pieces of pumpkin pie, graced with Cool Whip, floating in the sky. The slogan: "A Thanksgiving treat so good it flys." Someone forgot to tell the copywriter that verbs ending in "y" preceded by a consonant take an "ies" in plural: fly/flies.

• An ad for a well-known Scotch exhorted the public to "Give a gift that's been laying around for twelve years." What in the world does a gift lay? Golden gift eggs? The substitution of "laying" for "lying" is becoming more and more common in spoken English.

❋**Goofy Goof:** He waived his hands.

Still, seeing it in the pages of the *New Yorker*—even in an advertisement in the *New Yorker*—left me disheartened.

• A current radio ad for an eyeglass company goes: "Get your own pair of glasses 'cause these ones are mine." This jingle pains the Grammar Lady's sensitive ears. We can say, "I want these/those." When pointing to puppies in a window, we may tell the pet store clerk, "I want these furry ones," or "I want those furry ones." But we cannot say "these ones" or "those ones" and claim to be using correct grammar.

• A reader objected to a cornflakes ad that read, "Taste them again for the very first time." How can that be possible? We can't do something both "again" and "for the very first time." Unless, of course, this was poetry. Then I could let it go as a rather clever oxymoron.

• Why is the word *home* so frequently substituted for the word *house* these days? A house is merely a structure: it doesn't become your home until you actually move in. However, real estate agents, wanting to evoke an image of warmth and hospitality, never refer to the structures they're showing you as mere houses—they're always homes.

• Advertisements also often misuse the word *fun*. For example, a TV commercial for a particular lawn mower uses the phrase "so fun to run." The word *fun* is a noun, not an adjective, and should not be used in this manner. Unfortunately, the manufacturer probably thought that the grammatically correct phrase "so much fun to run" ruined the cadence of his jingle.

OF QUACKS AND MACS

Sometimes, even the Grammar Lady is willing to allow a lapse in language use if she deems the advertising campaign clever enough.

The Cadillac Catera uses a duck as its logo. Why, I cannot quite fathom. Regardless, one ad was introduced with the phrase "Duck Logic." It continued, "Ducks think differently than you and me." A reader called up to complain about this ad. She had been taught that the phrase should be: "Ducks think differently than you and I (do)."

In any case, ducks undoubtedly think differently than you and I. Still, I believe that Cadillac introduced the Catera, in part, to shed the company's dusty image. It tries to position the product as "youthful" and "fun" (the advertiser's words). Therefore, I'm guessing that the ad agency knew the grammar was wrong, but chose it anyway because it sounds much less formal than standard English.

Apple Computer has also annoyed some folks with its use of the word *different* and questionable grammar. "Think Different," the new Mac slogan goes. One caller thought it should run, "Think Differently." As a devout Macophile, I'm giving the company a bit of a break. "Think Different" means to think of something that is not usually thought of. If the ad agency had put a dash to indicate a hesitation that you'd hear in speech, I think it would be fine. In general, we need the adjective by the noun and the adverb, the *-ly* form, to follow a verb. *This is different technology; we must think differently about it.*

STORE WARS

Reader beware: I am going to bring up the infamous apostrophe again.

In the windows of Kaufmann's department store, I saw a display of evening clothes accompanied by signs reading "Night's Out." What can this possibly mean? "The night is out?" Where did it go? Surely, the department store meant "Nights Out." I called the store advertising people, who at first thought it might be a brand of clothing for fancy dress, but no one called back to follow up. Anyway, I took one look at these signs, and chose to do my holiday shopping elsewhere.

I do not mean to seem like a curmudgeon, but I had faced one too many misuses of the apostrophe that week. My readers understand the feeling. They're constantly feeding examples to me. Some of my favorite least-favorite uses:

• From a local floral shop: Boss's remember your secretaries this week.

• From a New York City supermarket ad: Whats For Dinner; Brauers Best Turkey Breast; Stouffers French Bread Pizza; Lemon's. (This one is almost endearing. If it weren't for the lemon, one would be tempted to give the store the benefit of the doubt in assuming they simply ran out of apostrophes, much the way they so often run out of whatever is on special.)

While we're in the supermarket, consider this item, culled from my local newspaper: "An average of 39 shopping carts is stolen from American supermarkets each hour." This sentence is grammatically incorrect. Can you guess why, apart from the moral issue? A general rule of thumb: When the word *average* is preceded by the word *a* or *an,* it takes a plural verb. The best way to have expressed the shopping-cart issue is: "An average of 39 shopping carts are stolen . . ." If, however, the word *average* is preceded by the word *the,* it takes a singular verb. "The average number of shopping carts stolen is . . ." The same rule holds true for the words *number* and *total.*

Some other issues arising from the retail world:

• "Bring" and "take" cause a lot of confusion. One reader wanted to know if there had been a change in language usage because the signs in her grocery store read, "Bring your produce to . . ." The general rule is that if you can substitute "go" in the verb part of the sentence, use "take." If you can substitute "come," use "bring." My reader should "go" to the clerk (with her produce).

• When clerks in department stores approach customers, the clerk says, "Did you need any help?" A reader wanted to know why they use the past tense; she needs help now, not yesterday. I reminded her that it's just a formula to ask if help is needed—it doesn't have anything to do with the past tense. What does "hello" mean? I also reminded her we should all be so lucky to have a clerk offer help in the first place.

QUESTIONS OF COMMERCE

Many of my readers have questions about the correct use of grammar as it applies to the world of commerce. A letter from a well-

Goofy Goof: On a nationally televised program on the state of American education, the experts were identified by name and position. One of the captions read "School Superintendant."

known software company read: "Sorry for the delay in sending this but as I explained, we obsoleted this line of software four years ago." Obsoleted? At first I was amazed by this seeming grammatical nonsense. But then the Grammar Lady herself learned a little something. I looked up this term, and found it has a venerable history. It dates from the late sixteenth century, and means, "to make obsolete by replacing with something newer and better; antiquate." I still don't like it much, though.

Speaking of incendiary matters, how can "inflammable" and "flammable" both mean to catch on fire easily? Both words do, in fact, mean likely to catch on fire. "Inflammable" (from the word *inflame*) was once used as the standard. However, some people confused the "in" prefix with the one meaning "not," as in "inhumane," and took inflammable to mean "not combustible." So "flammable" replaced the older form on the sides of trucks or containers of things easily set on fire.

One ardent fan wanted me to use my influence to get the local papers to spell the word *collectibles* correctly instead of their usual custom of printing "collectables." Unfortunately, sometimes even the Grammar Lady has to admit defeat. This is one such instance. The able/ible endings cause a lot of problems because the vowels sound alike, but "able" seems to be more popular. A 1951 collegiate dictionary lists both spellings as acceptable. Since dictionary revision lags behind popular changes in the language by quite a few years, I'm afraid this battle is lost.

Is there a free lunch? I do not know, but I do know whether or not such a thing would be complimentary or complementary. Think

PAROXYSM (puh-ROCK-siz-um) n. A sudden violent outburst; a fit of violent action or emotion. *The basketball team lost by one point, sending the coach into a paroxysm of rage.*

of "gift" and use the same vowel, *i*—complimentary. Meanwhile, anyone interested in free lunches might want to know which of the following is correct. "You may request my help to affect (make a difference in) collection of the debt." (I have a great many wealthy friends who owe me favors.) "You may request my help to effect (bring about) collection of the debt." (I'm the sheriff and I can put people in jail if they don't pay.)

The choice between "that" and "which" troubles many people, especially in writing where the meaning can change dramatically by using the wrong word. Once again, we turn to computers to clarify our position. "The computer, which proved too confusing for me to use, was returned to the store." Clauses beginning with "which" are set off by commas and contain extra, but not crucial, information. "I tried out two computers last week. The one that was too hard to master I left on the shelf. I purchased the other one." Clauses beginning with "that" contain identifying information and are not set off by commas.

Here's an etymological question to spice up this section of the book. Why is the union of truck drivers called the "teamsters"? It goes back to when hired drivers of teams of horses or other animals were called teamsters. This is an interesting example of language stability; even though the activity is totally different and the word no longer evokes images of teams of animals, the word has retained the meaning of "hired driver."

WORRISOME WORD

SARDONIC (sar-DON-ik) adj. Characterized by bitter or scornful derision; mocking; cynical; sneering. *"And where did your campaign funds come from?" asked the Senator, sardonically.*

CROSS-CULTURAL COMMERCE

American grammar and mores can often confuse persons from other cultures.

A foreign student of the English language recently wrote to ask why checkout clerks so often pose the question "Paper or plastic?" I explained that, in the United States, items can be taken home in paper bags, or plastic ones. This answer drew a major rebuke from a horrified reader. "Well, you really fouled up big time last week on that 'paper or plastic' answer," she wrote. "I've been in grocery stores all over this country, and everyone knows the cashier is asking about the method of payment when they ask the question— paper money or credit card." I disagreed, and, as it happened, we had a houseguest over the holidays who held a summer job as a cashier in a grocery store. I put the question to her. She laughed and said, "Of course it's the bags. A lot of times we don't even ask the paper-or-plastic question until after the customer has paid."

A British reader posed this question: "When we go to banks we have to queue up waiting for our turn. Usually, we get a number from a machine that dispenses numbers in sequence. Can we call such numbers 'Queue Numbers'?" I replied that, in the United States, we have no specific term for this. There is usually a sign over the device saying "Take a number," and the clerks change the number on a big board at the back of the area. It doesn't happen in banks here, but in bakeries or the deli section of grocery stores. Wouldn't it be a great idea in doctors' waiting rooms? (See chapter 9.)

VICTORIES IN THE GRAMMAR WARS

After all this carping, we really do need to applaud good deeds in the commercial world.

In a national ad campaign for a gasoline company one character reads a book to another, who promptly falls asleep. The closing line is "Now I gotta lie him down someplace." The Grammar Lady felt it her duty to call the gasoline company to complain, incurring a long-distance telephone charge in the process. And, of course, her telephone call was not answered by a real person, but by an answering machine. A company representative did return my call, however. He apologized for getting the verb wrong. He said the mistake occurred because it was ad-libbed during taping and had never appeared in a typed script. It turns out that I was not the only one who complained, so maybe the company will be more careful in the future. Either way, the callback gave me heart. I began to believe protest might not be as futile as we sometimes think.

The pasta pickle proved it. In a recent commercial for a canned pasta product, a well-dressed young mother said, "Me and Patsy take turns with each other's kids . . ." I sent the company a letter of complaint. They changed the ad to "Celeste and I take care of each other's kids." Two corrections for the price of one stamp!

Have you ever noticed the grocery store checkout signs that read "Eight items or less"? If you can count the objects denoted, you should say "fewer." Wegman's grocery stores in upstate New York use the correct phrasing. So do Giant Eagle stores in Pittsburgh and Andronico's in Berkeley, California. Giant Eagle recently renovated the signs after years of using the incorrect phrase. I called one of the company's district managers to congratulate him, and asked why the signs were changed. He laughed and said he really didn't know. I'll gladly take the credit after years of peaceful protest. This question was the item they used on *Hollywood Squares*. If they show the rerun often enough, maybe other markets will see the light.

DON'T SUE US!

American society has become so litigious that American business goes to great lengths to protect itself from possible product-liability suits. Lee Ellis, one of the first Recreational Grammarians on the Grammar Lady Web site, offers the following list of warnings and chuckles.

- On a Sears hair dryer: Do not use while sleeping.
- On packaging for a Rowenta Iron: Do not iron clothes on body.
- On Nytol (a sleep aid): Warning: may cause drowsiness. (Could we sue if it didn't?)
- On Marks & Spencer Bread Pudding: Product will be hot after heating.
- On Sainsbury's Peanuts: Warning: Contains nuts.
- On a chainsaw: Do not attempt to stop chain with your hands.
- On a kitchen knife: Warning: Keep out of children.

Perhaps the only thing funnier than consumer warnings are consumer directions.

- On a bar of Dial soap: Directions: Use like regular soap.
- On some Swann frozen dinners: Serving suggestion: Defrost.
- On a hotel-provided shower cap in a box: Fits one head.
- On the bottom of a box of Tesco's Tiramisú dessert: Do not turn upside down.

Then there are the ones that teenagers would greet with "Well, duh!"

- On Boot's Children's Cough Medicine: Do not drive car or operate machinery.
- On a bag of Fritos: You could be a winner! No purchase necessary. Details inside.
- On a string of Christmas lights: For indoor or outdoor use only.
- On a food processor: Not to be used for the other use.
- On an American Airlines packet of nuts: Instructions: open packet, eat nuts. (In the nut-free zone, of course.)

Grammar Points

that/which
flammable/inflammable
collectible/able
an/the average + verb agreement
lie X down
like/as
teamsters
complimentary/complementary
the/a number
here's/are
house/home
a/an + vowel sound
adverb placement
these ones
Me & X + verb
lay/lie
than I/me
think different/ly
"Did you need help?"

affect/effect
so fun
bring/take

THE QUIZZICAL I

On the basis of the meaning of the sentence, decide if the verb derives from *lay* or *lie*.

1. Pittsburgh lies at the head of the Ohio River.

2. She laid the rumor to rest at last.

3. Did you lay the papers where he can find them?

4. The leaves have lain in their yard for months.

5. The workers have laid the foundation for the new terminal.

6. She lay down for a rest before the children came home.

7. The empty trash cans have been lying at the curb for days.

8. When will they be laying the floor?

9. He had the habit of lying in a hammock on Sunday afternoons.

10. She laid the baby next to the puppy for the photograph.

Typo of the Weak

From a West Coast–based national association's Washington, D.C., chapter's monthly electronic news bulletin, it brings new meaning to the term "just blowin' through."

Association President [Harvey Smedlap and wife, Semantha] jetted in from California to be overnight gusts at the White House.

Typo of the Weak

From a Washington State weekly financial publication. Hey, if at first you don't succeed.

Immediately following his company's bankruptcy proceedings, he reigned as CEO.

Chapter Eleven

Bets and Arguments, Cries and Whispers

So, did you happen to catch Super Bowl XXXII between the Broncos and the Packers? We gave up on the game after the half, but we recorded all the ads. I almost turned it off before the National Anthem. Madden or Sommerall (I can never tell their voices apart because I don't watch) intoned "The National Anthem will be sang by Cher." A few days after the game I was interviewed on a local TV show and a couple of Canadian radio stations; the anecdote was received with shocked looks and gasps. I could see they didn't believe me. Made me wish we had taped more than the ads.

Now at least I understand why people use the Hotline so much for settling bets and arguments. To tell you the truth it makes me feel somewhat hopeful—if people still care enough about the rightness of language to call someone to ask, maybe there's a chance. On the other hand, what do we make of folks calling a stranger on an 800 number? I always try to claim a piece of the action when the caller mentions money, but I haven't cashed in yet.

Here's a typical exchange:

CALLER: Hi, Grammar Lady. What is the possessive of knife? Is it knife's, e.g., "The knife's edge was shining through the darkness"? I've got a $100 ridin' on it! Thanks a lot!

ME: Right. What's my cut? Actually it should be the edge of the knife. But for betting purposes "knife's" will do.

FRIENDS AND FAMILY FEUDS

A gloomy gray Sunday afternoon in Pittsburgh and no more football. Just me, my computer, and the unrelenting ringing of the Grammar Hotline. Thirty-five calls so far and it's only 5:30 P.M. Who do they think is going to answer a grammar question on Sunday? Heaven help me tomorrow. Maybe I'll surprise everyone and take the day off.

One caller asked about phone etiquette. When someone asks, "How are you?" the caller customarily answers, "I am fine, thank you." However, many of her educated friends respond, "I am well." She wonders if one form is preferred. Both are acceptable responses to the question; the response to avoid, of course, is "I am good."

A couple wanted me to settle an argument. When they play cards, the wife says, "Spades is trump," but her husband says, "Spades are trump." According to the unabridged dictionary I use, both are correct. That kind of solution is gratifying.

It's not always quite so easy. A woman complained that her husband often says, "I'm going outside to mow lawn." She told him that it should be "the lawn," but she wanted me to mediate. I would say "the lawn" but wondered if it might be a regional dialect variation. Then she had a second question about how many days until Christmas. When counting down the days until Christmas, say it's December 3, there would be twenty-two days until Christmas. Her husband said that is incorrect, there would be only twenty-one days until Christmas, because you don't count Christmas Day. I agreed with the husband on that one. Makes me wonder if I should go into the marital counseling business.

On a number of occasions, a man asked his wife if she had "rewound" a videotape. After saying this word, there came moments of ridicule and debate on whether this is proper English. I wondered what she thought it should be. The past and past participle of "wind" is "wound," although the dictionary lists a (rare) "winded." There is no reason to think the addition of the prefix *re-* would change the base verb.

I was asked to settle an argument between a woman and her friend. She said, "I'm going to put a lamp on either side of the sofa." The woman asked, "Which side?" The friend looked at her as if she had gone crazy. She claimed that "on either side" means both sides. While "on each side" or "on both sides" might be more precise, I certainly understand this sentence to mean there will be two lamps. Incidentally, to make certain that the interior decorator and I do not share some idiosyncratic dialect, I asked several other people, all of whom agreed with our interpretation.

Another minor dispute involved someone who grew up hearing and saying that it will be "bitter cold" tonight. Now he hears many weather forecasters saying it will be "bitterly cold." He thought that "bitter cold" sounded as if it could be from Shakespeare. I never did check into that. Bitter is both an adjective, meaning having an acrid taste, and an adverb, meaning exceedingly or extremely. Thus, bitter cold is correct. It's been in the language since Old and Middle English and was available to Shakespeare. "Bitterly cold" is what we linguists call a "hypercorrection."

Recently, a group of friends got into a discussion about which is correct: beer or beers? It had been a habit of the caller's to say that he just had three beers, but a friend continued to say he had three beer. "Beer" can refer to a single beer or to the subject of beer in general. However, when one is talking about three separate bottles or mugs of beer, one would definitely say, "I had three beers."

During the holidays I received an urgent request for assistance in winning a bet and protecting this guy's pride. Macho stuff. He had promised a group that he could get an answer to a grammar question using nothing more than the Internet. Here's the scenario. His last name was "Brees." He was writing a holiday letter and wished to sign it, "From the Brees_____." Here's the question. Should it be "Breeses," plural, or should it be "Brees'," the possessive? He had found a *lot* of references to the "it's" issue, but nothing to the name issue. I sent him a message via E-mail: Breeses!!!!

DO NOT PUT AN APOSTROPHE IN YOUR NAME SIGN OR ON YOUR HOLIDAY CARDS!!!

I asked him to let me know who won the bet. He did, of course, but his wife, not quite willing to concede complete defeat, ordered the Christmas card pictures with "From the Brees Family." Now that's a clever way to avoid the issue altogether. At least they didn't send out a grammatically incorrect holiday card. (I warned you I would get this into every chapter.)

Someone's wife and kids constantly use "further" when talking about distances. He tells them that they should use "farther," and can't persuade them that they are wrong. They even contend Webster supports their position. When I was growing up, we remembered this as far = distance; therefore, farther for distances. Alas, this has changed so that "farther" and "further" are both used for distance, but only "further" is used to mean "additional."

Two friends were having a debate about whether there can be grammatically correct double negatives. One said that "does not decrease" and "I can't stop" are double negatives, but the other disagrees. The sentences mentioned are not double negatives even though "decrease" and "stop" have some negative connotation. "We don't have no paper" and "He hasn't never been to Paris" are true double negatives, in which two negative elements appear in the verb part of the sentence.

Some friends were arguing whether "Xerox copy" is redundant, as is "Kleenex tissue." For many years the Xerox Corporation strove to prevent the eponymous (common, lowercase) use of its brand name. Every time they saw a printed piece with the name used as a verb or noun, the attorneys would fire off a warning. Perhaps the Xerox minions still do this for written misuses of their brand name, but they can't police people's speech. A lot of people now use Xerox, Kleenex, Rollerblade, and other brand names as lowercase nouns or verbs.

Believe it or not people sometimes call the Grammar Hotline with questions not directly related to grammar. A woman in central Pennsylvania was having a disagreement with her husband. She wanted to know the difference between a metaphor and a simile. A simile is a comparison using "like" or "as." *A smile as beautiful as a summer's day.* A metaphor is comparison without "like" or "as." *My love is a red, red rose.* I think she needs to upgrade her family dictionary.

The other evening some friends were discussing several desserts. One said a particular cake was "more sweet" than the other. The caller commented that it had to be "sweeter." She was right. This use of "more" to make adjectives comparative, rather than adding the suffix -*er*, seems to be a trend of some kind. We may need to get the Grammar sociologists to keep an eye on this one.

WORRISOME WORD

MAUNDER (rhymes with launder) v. To talk aimlessly or foolishly; to go in an aimless or confused manner. *Many people seem to be maundering through life these days, without goals or ambitions.*

As I write, the congressional hearings on a certain infamous end-of-the-millennium scandal are creating a lot of dissension—even on language use. We hear things such as, "I would ask the gentleman so and so." Would ask? Why don't they just ask? I don't have any idea why they use four or five words where one would do just as well. My question is why they all ask the same questions over and over. Don't they listen to one another? Probably not. Here is a prime example of language used not to communicate ideas, but to promote some self-aggrandizing agenda. If it does nothing more than incite a taxpayers' revolt, the coverage of these inane hearings will at least have done some good.

Congress reminds me of filibusters and speeches and a heavy bet a man had with his mother-in-law about whether one could write as well as speak extemporaneously. According to the usage notes in my unabridged dictionary, the answer is yes. Essay exams and writing tests in job interviews are good examples of extemporaneous writing.

DISSENSION IN THE RANKS

Split infinitives seem to cause a lot of distress. When I posted a list of frequently asked questions on my Web site, no question got as much attention as this one—60,000 or so hits, whereas the others might have received a couple of thousand.

A caller was wedged between grammar rules and conventions at the office. She knew better than to split an infinitive when the result is an awkward sentence, but wondered if it was ever permissible to split an infinitive, e.g., ". . . to help you to better understand the material . . ." When the grammar rules of English were first formulated, they were based on Latin, a language in which it is not possible to split an infinitive because infinitives themselves are single words.

While finicky purists still insist on the rule, most users would agree with you that splitting is not wrong if it does not result in an awkward construction. In fact, the modern saying "To err is human; to really foul up, use a computer" wouldn't be as effective without splitting "to foul up." Besides, late in 1998 the *Oxford Dictionary* folks decreed that splitting infinitives is no longer a grammar crime.

Some workers were having a debate about whether to use "strong" or "strongly" in this sentence. The people who vote for "strong" say there is a rule that the *-ly* forms are wrong after verbs like "feel." "Our company feels strong/ly about this issue." They are partly right. When the verb expresses a sense of health and refers to the subject, we use only the adjectives: I feel strong because I have been working out. (Other verbs like this are look, taste, smell, seem, sound.) In the example above the meaning is different—it means "to believe"—and does not refer to the subject, so "strongly" is correct.

Two colleagues, a male and female, had a long-standing bet (with great stakes). They wanted help in correctly punctuating the trademark name "Peel and Shield."

1. Peel 'n Shield
2. Peel 'n' Shield
3. Peel-n-Shield

They even threw in a wild card, for what reason, I have no idea. At the risk of causing another Toys Я Us, I have to go with Peel 'n' Shield since they left off a letter on each end. The man won the bet, and said his colleague was quite bitter. It must have been pretty intense because I then got a message from the colleague saying that she was not so much bitter, but smothering in the land of gloating. Not only that, the war was not over. It never ceases to amaze and amuse me how heated these disputes can get. Maybe we have hit on the root of the dismay people feel when their language is corrected. Or maybe it's just another skirmish in the Battle of the Sexes.

A caller and his boss have a difference of opinion regarding the use of the following form: *He graduated college.* He believes that the standard, preferred use is *He graduated from college.* The boss insists that "graduated college" is an acceptable regional variation. He knew that she would win this argument because she is the boss. But he wanted to know who was right. He was. Come to think of it, when men call for arbitration on things like this, they almost always frame the question in terms of some kind of competition. Women, on the other hand, seek more often to vindicate themselves. I'm not really sure what that tells us. Maybe nothing, but it's worth a passing thought. When I get time, I'll give it one.

Another office worker had a small battle with his manager regarding the word *myself* in the sentences *Thank you for meeting with Bob and me* versus *Thank you for meeting with Bob and myself.* He believed that the former is correct and wanted me to clarify the correct usage and cite the grammatical rule. He had been unable to find a reference in Strunk and White or other handbooks in his office. Strunk and White does not cover this because it was not a common error when that book was written. If he removes "Bob and" from the sentence, he will see that "me" is the correct response.

There was a little preholiday dispute going on at work. At lunch one day the folks brought back to the office many ketchup packets and spread them on the desk. One colleague looked at the packets and said, "Wow, look at all those ketchups!" This began a bitter

WORRISOME WORD

TORPID (TORE-pid) adj. Having lost motion or the power of exertion; lethargic, sluggish, dopey. *The thought of the upcoming hot, humid days makes me torpid already.*

argument over whether the collection of packets should be referred to as "ketchup" or "ketchups." One side cited examples such as shrimp, deer, and fish, claiming that "ketchup" falls in a category with these words in which the plural form does not end with an *s*. After a little research someone discovered from the *World Wide Webster's Dictionary* that "shrimps," "deers," and "fishes" are all valid words. However, there was no information regarding the plural form of "ketchup." These people simply did not have enough to do. I gave little credence to a source that says "shrimps, etc." are valid words. Ketchup, like "milk," is a mass or noncount noun that usually does not have a plural form ending in "s." Most mass nouns are made plural by adding a thing that can be counted—bottles of milk/packets of ketchup. What I'm really longing to know is what they were planning to do with all those ketchups!

A friend and co-worker insisted that the word *artist* does not acquire an "s" in the plural form when the fields of artistry are the same. The caller believed that it gets an "s" just as many other words do in the plural. (One artist, two artists.) While I do not understand the proviso about the "fields of artistry," artist is made plural with an *s*.

PLURAL PLURALITY

There's no help for it. I'm afraid this is where I have to break down and list a lot of strange and wonderful rules for forming plurals.

Nouns Without Plural Forms (Mass Nouns)

Some nouns do not usually have plural forms: furniture, silver, music, homework, milk, information. The words are made plural by adding a phrase: two cartons of milk.

Plural of Nouns

There are three simple rules for making nouns (including names) plural.

1. Add *s*: book/books, house/houses, piano/pianos, John/Johns
2. Add *es* if the word ends in *s/sh/ch/x/z*: census/censuses, bush/bushes, church/churches, Rex/Rexes
3. If the noun ends in *y* preceded by a consonant, change *y* to *i* and add *es*: fly/flies, lady/ladies, salary/salaries. If the *y* is preceded by a vowel, the regular rule applies—add *s*: days, boys, journeys. Proper nouns simply add *s*: Marys, the Kelleys, two Germanys

Singular Nouns That End in *S*

Some nouns, such as news, seem to be plural because they end in *s*, but they are singular: "The news is good this week." Other words like this include the names for diseases: measles, mumps; some games: darts, checkers, dominoes; and subject areas: mathematics, linguistics.

Plural Nouns Without Singular Forms

There are two types of nouns that don't normally have singular forms.

❋**Goofy Goof:** In a recent issue of my favorite financial paper this appears: In a telephone call with an important client, the phone suddenly went dead. It turned out that one of the callers "had chewed through the chord."

1. Clothing and tools that consist of two attached parts, such as scissors. "The scissors are in the drawer." These nouns can be made singular by adding a phrase: "I need a pair of scissors." (Note: pair is plural in the regular way—two pairs of pants.) Other nouns like this are

binoculars	scales	tongs
glasses	shears	trousers
pajamas	shorts	tweezers
pants	suspenders	
pliers	tights	

2. The nouns below are usually in the plural form. When they are singular the meaning changes as in "Her looks are spoiled by her personality. The look she gave me would stop a train."

amends	clothes	regards	riches
annals	contents	odds	suds
archives	earnings	outskirts	surroundings
arms (guns)	fireworks	premises	thanks
arrears	funds	stairs	troops
auspices	pains (take)	remains	valuables
ashes	looks	means	wages
bowels	manners	savings	wits

Compound Nouns

Compound nouns have two (or more) elements, sometimes hyphenated. There are three ways to make them plural.

1. Plural in the first element

attorney general = attorneys general
grant-in-aid = grants-in-aid
man-of-war = men-of-war
mother-in-law = mothers-in-law
notary public = notaries public
passerby = passersby

2. Plural in first and last

gentleman farmer = gentlemen farmers
woman doctor = women doctors

3. Plural in last element (most common)

breakdowns	fountain pens	spoonfuls
forget-me-nots	mouthfuls	take-offs

Irregular Plurals

Most of the words with irregular plurals are so common that they are not a problem (loaf/loaves, child/children, woman/women, mouse/mice), but there are a few common ones that cause difficulties, especially in spelling.

1. Nouns that end in *o*

- Usually add *s*—piano/pianos
- Can add *s* or *es*—banjos/banjoes

archipelago	halo
buffalo	tornado
cargo	volcano
flamingo	motto

• Add *es*

echoes	tomatoes
embargoes	torpedoes
heroes	vetoes
potatoes	

2. Nouns that have only one form: sheep, deer, species, Chinese

3. Nouns that end in *us*

• Plural ends in *i*

stimulus/stimuli
bacillus/bacilli
locus/loci

• Plural ends in either *i* or *es*—cactus = cacti/cactuses

focus	radius
fungus	terminus
nucleus	syllabus

• Plural ends in *es*—bonus/bonuses

apparatus	circus
campus	prospectus
census	virus

Confusing words: alumnus (man), alumni (men), alumna (woman), alumnae (women). My advice: use graduate and graduates. And no, you can't be an alumnus if you attended the school but did not graduate.

4. Nouns that end in *a*

- Plural ends in *ae*—alga/algae, larva/larvae
- Plural ends in *ae* or *s*—formula, formulae/formulas

antenna
nebula
vertebra

- Plural ends in *s*—area, areas

arena	diploma
dilemma	drama

5. Nouns that end in *um*

- Plural ends in a—addendum, addenda

bacterium, bacteria	stratum, strata
erratum, errata	datum, data

- Plural ends in *a* or *s*—aquarium, aquaria/aquariums

medium
memorandum
symposium

- Plural ends in *s*—stadium, stadiums

album
forum
museum
ultimatum

6. Nouns that end in *is*

- Plural ends in *es*—basis, bases (pronounced *seez*)

<table>
<tr><td>analysis</td><td>hypothesis</td></tr>
<tr><td>axis</td><td>oasis</td></tr>
<tr><td>crisis</td><td>synopsis</td></tr>
<tr><td>diagnosis</td><td>thesis</td></tr>
</table>

- Plural is regular—metropolis, metropolises

7. Nouns that end in *ex* or *ix*

- Plural ends *ices* (pronounced *ih-ceez*) or regular *es*—index, indices/indexes

<table>
<tr><td>apex</td><td>matrix</td></tr>
<tr><td>appendix</td><td>vortex</td></tr>
</table>

8. Nouns ending in *on*

- Plural ends in *a*—criterion, criteria; phenomenon, phenomena
- Plural is regular—electron, electrons; proton, protons

Plurals of Letters and Numbers

The authorities differ on this topic, so use the style book for your professional area. Until quite recently it was the vogue to add an apostrophe followed by an *s*—A's, 1990's. Now it's more common to see them without the apostrophe—1990s. I think it is easier to understand with the apostrophe, but the key is to be consistent.

PUT YOUR PUNCTUATION WHERE YOUR PAUSE IS

Some coworkers were having a debate. One says the standards have changed and now one space after the period at the end of a sentence is appropriate. The friend says that nothing has changed and that there are still two spaces after every period. Except in typing class, there never were two spaces after a period; one is appropriate.

There was a debate in an office concerning the correct usage of hyphens.

1. Arrangements are placed with well established, highly rated reinsurers.
2. Arrangements are placed with well-established, highly rated reinsurers.
3. Arrangements are placed with well established, highly-rated reinsurers.
4. Arrangements are placed with well-established, highly-rated reinsurers.

And the envelope, please. The winner is number two, well-established only. When the adverb ends in ly, there is no hyphen.

Folks around the water cooler have been arguing about questions and quotations since the beginning of, well, water coolers. Look at this sentence: "Do you want one scoop of ice cream or two?" Does the question mark belong inside the quotes or outside? Inside. If the quoted material and the entire sentence each require the same mark of punctuation, use only one mark—the one that comes first.

For punctuation with quoted words, follow the conventions of American printers:

1. Place the period and the comma always within the quotation marks.
2. Place the colon and semicolon always outside the quotation marks.
3. Place the dash, question mark, and exclamation mark within the quotation marks when they apply only to the quoted matter; place them outside when they apply to the whole sentence.

PONDERING PRONUNCIATION

Many Americans are fearful that they are going to say something wrong. I really need to investigate the root of this insecurity, but that's another volume. For now we'll look at some of the more common sources of potential bets and arguments.

✳**Goofy Goof:** This comes from a description of a wedding gift of a honeymoon crossing of the Atlantic on one of the ocean liners. An uncle came to the "ceremony with a pair of first-class births on the Queen . . ."

Someone called to ask the correct pronunciation of the word *catsup*. His grandmother had instructed him to say it this way. "Catsup" is a variant spelling for the more common "ketchup," which is pronounced "catchup." The condiment and the word were introduced to English speakers in Malaysia in the early 1700s. Depending on the language of origin, the word was pronounced "catsup" or "ketchup," with the resulting variant spellings. So the grandson and grandmother can live in harmony on this one. Either is correct.

A reader was taught that the word *coupon* was pronounced "coo-pon" and not "q-pon." Her Webster's dictionary shows that the coo pronunciation of the word is correct. She wanted to know why intelligent and well-educated people continue to mispronounce it. Having grown up with q-pon immediately put me at a disadvantage in this discussion, since I like to consider myself "intelligent and well educated." In any case, the *Random House Dictionary* lists both pronunciations as completely standard, although it notes that the *q* variety is often criticized, probably because the French origin would normally preclude the *q* pronunciation. There are regional variations in the pronunciation of American English, and this may be an example of one of them.

Some folks were having a dispute about the proper pronunciation of the word *primer*. If the meaning is a book for beginning readers, the pronunciation is PRIM-er. If it is a base coat of paint on a bare surface, it's PRIME-er; so both sides are right as long as the proper pronunciation is applied to the correct definition.

There was a lot of money riding on my answer to this question. Someone said the word that means one's strong point (forte) is pronounced FOR-tay. I was sorry to disappoint, but the word is correctly pronounced to rhyme with "short." "For-TAY" means "loud" in musical terms. I've heard that people will bet on strange things, but this is a new one on me. This distinction may soon disappear, however. My favorite talk show host is just such a person as I have mentioned—forties, well-educated, and very articulate. On Tuesdays her sister in the Midwest joins her on the show for an hour. On one occasion they discussed this pair of words, got the meanings right but concluded that no one uses them correctly, so they misuse them too because people would think that they are wrong if they used them correctly!!! Maybe I've been wrong about the whole thing; it's not ignorance, but the fear of being different that drives these boomers. Might I suggest the use of "strong suit" instead of an erroneous usage.

A caller's friend chided him for pronouncing the "t" in often. He complained that she *offen* does things like that! This is a word that has changed in my lifetime. We learned it in school as a "sight word—the *t* is silent." About ten years ago I went to a lecture where the academic used the word often and pronounced the *t* every time. I stopped listening to the lecture and counted the occurrences of the word. Imagine my chagrin at finding the *t* pronunciation sitting alongside my *t*-less one in the modern dictionaries. I have bowed gracefully to this change, but I still keep my pronunciation.

Someone wanted to know the correct spelling and pronunciation for the ice cream–like dessert. Sherbet? Sherbert? He always swore that it can be spelled "sorbet" but everybody thought he was nuts.

WORRISOME WORD

ICONOCLAST (eye-KAHN-uh-klast) n. A breaker of images, especially those set up for religious veneration; a person who attacks cherished beliefs as being erroneous. *People who propose new ideas such as abolishing slavery, or suffrage for women, are often seen as iconoclasts because they support change in the foundation of the society.*

Well, there's sorbet, pronounced sore-BAY, which seems to be taking the place of old standby sherbet (SHUR-bit).

Should words like cliché, café, attaché, and the like, continue to have the foreign accents and circumflexes when used in English? Is the case the same for handwritten compositions and typed compositions, as a rule? And what happens to the pronunciation of these words? For instance, should "café" be pronounced with one syllable or two? These burning issues were bothering certain callers. My *Random House Unabridged Dictionary* prints the acute (´) accent on each of the words in question, so I guess we should include the marks in our spellings. The pronunciation remains the same.

On that note, I would bid you *à tout à l'heure* if I could only find those darn accent marks on my computer.

Grammar Points

pronunciation
  catsup
  coupon
  primer
  forte
  often
  sherbet
  words with acute accents
I'm good/well
spades is/are trump
speak/write extemporaneously
rewind/rewound
either side of the sofa
bitter(ly) cold
plural—beer
name sign apostrophe

farther/further
double negatives
redundancy of eponyms (Kleenex tissue)
metaphor/simile
sweeter/more sweet
would ask
split infinitives
feel strong(ly)
graduate from college
plural of ketchup
plural of mass nouns
like/as
plural—artist
plural formation
spaces after period
hyphens in compound adjectives
quotation marks and question marks
quotation marks and other punctuation
quiz
plural formation

MARY'S KILLER BEE

With one exception, this set of words appeared in *Esquire* in 1967 as a test of the twenty most frequently misspelled words and later was reprinted in the *Reader's Digest*. See if you can choose the correct spelling of each word. Don't look before you try. There is no tangible reward for getting them right—just the comforting knowledge that you don't have to rely on your computer spell checker. The definition is first.

1. To make liquid.
   liquify / liquefy / liquiefy

2. Foolish.
   asinine / assinine / asenine

3. Vivid reddish orange.
   vermillion / vurmilion / vermilion

4. Soft leather shoe.
   mocassin / moccasin / moccassin

5. A treatment to establish immunity.
   innoculation / inocculation / inoculation

6. Adapt.
   accommodate / acomodate / accomudate

7. Sponsor of entertainment.
   impressario / impresairio / impresario

8. Revive.
   resusitate / resuscitate / resussitate

9. Take the place of.
   supercede / superceed / supersede

10. Very ornate.
    rococo / roccoco / rococco

11. A large tent.
    pavilion / pavillion / pavilon

12. Make rare, thin, or less dense.
    rareify / rarefy / rarify

13. White sandwich spread.
    mayonaise / mayonese / mayonnaise

14. Accompanying musical part played by a single instrument.
    obbligato / obligato / obbligatto

15. Excite pleasurably.
    titillate / tittilate / titilate

16. Dehydrate.
    desicate / dessicate / desiccate

17. Violation of something sacred.
    sacrilegious / sacreligious / saccreligious

18. One who assumes an identity.
    imposster / impostor / immposter

19. Agreement in opinion.
    consensis / concensus / consensus

20. Tiny.
    minisqule / minuscule / minescule

PERFECTLY PUNCTUATED

Put punctuation marks where they should be.

1. The man asked, What's for dinner

2. I hate this place yelled Jenny.

3. Where did you find that old tape of *I Love Lucy*

4. The comic book store has lots of old copies of *Superman*

5. *Macbeth Hamlet Othello* and *Much Ado About Nothing* will be performed this year.

Typo of the Weak

From an ancient black-and-white viewgraph shown at a corporate presentation to top management comes this exceedingly rare typo: one legitimate word split into two legitimate words. How fortuitous that the three named execs, all watching the screen, happened to be wearing their brown slacks that day.

President and CEO [I. M. Topdoggie] has no trouble shooting executives like Smith, Jones, and Williams.

Typo of the Weak

Blown in from the Dakotas, a TV weather forecaster's brief graphic. We know that hot type has long since become history, but how about this publishing software's capabilities!

Cold font tonight.

Typo of the Weak

From a Maryland weekly's classified ad section header, a brief yet pungent statement. It beats—but not by much—having to take out the garage.

Garbage Sales

PART THREE

✳

Have We Lost Our Minds?

Chapter Twelve

Mail Call

These letters might not qualify as "saving the best for last," but I hope you will find them as fascinating as I did while I was composing my pithy answers.

Dear Grammar Lady,
How would I talk about myself in first person plural?

The only way I can think of to accomplish such a feat is to invent a new language. The first person plural pronoun is "we." But when you say "we," you talk about yourself and others. However, if you are a British royal, that doesn't really present a problem.

Dear Grammar Lady,
There was an article in the paper about a woman who wanted to improve the abysmal manners of service people who are rude and unhelpful. She mentioned doing away with "Machiavellian manners." What does that mean?

It means she doesn't know what "Machiavellian" means. Machiavellian is an adjective describing unscrupulous, dishonest, deceptive behavior designed to achieve one's ends. How this could be applied to discourteous service people is beyond me.

Dear Grammar Lady,
A friend introduced me to a new word she had heard from a radio newscaster: accessicity. e.g., "One must have accessicity to cash if one wants to buy a car."

It's amazing how many people don't know the basics; "accessicity" for "access" is pretty silly.

Dear Grammar Lady,
The following Monster Memo is quoted verbatim from a memo circulated at my friend's school.

SUBJECT: Supervision Area 11 has been assigned to each of you between respective periods. For clarification and placement purposes, please assume the position adjacent to refuge container. The placement intent is to allow visual sight of the walkways. Additionally, the placement provides individual visibility presence which will curtail problems.

This is a real puzzle. Do they provide translations?

Dear Grammar Lady,
If "roadhouse" is a compound noun, is a word like "carpet" also?

I take it that you mean "carpet" as in floor covering. The answer is no. A compound noun takes two words and combines their meanings into a new idea. A roadhouse is a building near a road, but "carpet" has nothing to do with cars or pets; it's coincidental that the two separate syllables have independent meanings.

Dear Grammar Lady,
This sentence sounds funny. What is wrong with it? "A vehicle was stolen at a rate of three per minute."

It sounds as if one car is being stolen over and over. To be grammatically accurate, the subject should be plural: vehicles were stolen . . .

Dear Grammar Lady,
Here's a message I got on my computer network. "So, without further adieu, the committee members are . . ."

"Adieu" for "ado" is not a very common substitution. It just goes to show that computers can't save us from ourselves. "Adieu," which is pronounced the same as ado, means good-bye or farewell. "I bid you adieu."

Dear Grammar Lady,
I belong to a group of crafters who sew. There was a suggestion in our national newsletter that we call ourselves sewers in the hope that the hyphen would distinguish us from "sewers" or storm drains, etc. I think it's ridiculous. What do you think?

I agree with you. There is a group of words, called "homographs," which are spelled alike but have different meanings. Usually the words have the same pronunciation. Ex: ball: a round object *or* a formal dance; *or* bark: tree covering *or* the

sound a dog makes. *A small subset have different pronuncia-*
tions, as in your example or bass: a fish, *and* bass: a low voice;
or bow: a weapon for shooting arrows, *or* bow: bend low in
respect. *As a rule the context tells us which meaning is neces-*
sary, and we don't even notice the other unless it is pointed out.
It seems odd that someone with your hobby would see the word
sewer *and think of underground drains.*

Dear Grammar Lady,
In some areas of the country, carbonated beverages are called
"pop." However, my son insists that Pepsi and ginger ale are
not included by this term. What do you think?

Since I originated in one of those parts of the country, I thought
I would know: certainly Pepsi and ginger ale are "pop." How-
ever, talking this over with other native "pop" speakers, it seems
there is disagreement. Everyone agrees that Pepsi is "pop," but
some people don't think ginger ale is. It seems to be in a cat-
egory that includes things like soda water and tonic.

Dear Grammar Lady,
On the green at the golf course, I spotted a ball. I inquired,
"Whose ball is that?" Someone in another group replied, "It is
I." Can this be a correct response to the question?

Not unless the person is pretending to have become the ball.
The expected response would be "It's mine." I think the other
golfer is pulling your leg.

Dear Grammar Lady,
Please tell us how to interpret the following: "No response will
be understood as a request to delete your name from the mailing list."

It turns the reader's expectations upside down. "No response will be" leads us to anticipate something like "neglected or overlooked." When we see "understood," we have to go back and reread. What is wrong with a straightforward "If you don't respond, your name will be deleted from the mailing list." It's three words shorter and much easier to understand.

Dear Grammar Lady,
A local service group sent a flyer saying "Piece of mind is just a few seconds away." Shouldn't that be "peace" as in peace and tranquility?

Yes, unless the group is holding some kind of fund-raiser by selling bits (pieces) of the members' minds.

Dear Grammar Lady,
I hate the growing usage of the word *axe* for *ask*. The TV talk shows are glutted with it. For instance, we hear "I axed him . . ." or "Let me axe him . . ." (No thanks, I'd prefer a lethal injection.) If we keep "axing" people at the rate we have been, we will end up a country of serial murderers. Is there a reason other than sloppiness that this change is happening?

How widespread is this? Do the hosts and the guests do it equally? Do the audience members do the "axing"? When assessing a potential language change, we need to know how widely imitated the users will be. If educated celebrity hosts and guests are doing it, they might be imitated by the audience and the viewers. If it is mainly audience members, the chance for imitation is less likely. In physiological terms, the past tense "axed" is easier to say than "asked," and pronunciation changes tend to favor ease of pronunciation.

Dear Grammar Lady,
My favorite phrase for illustrating the spoken English language concerns a situation that arose when some of my buddies were way back in the wilderness driving around looking for a place to stay. They knocked on the door of an old house along the road. An old bewhiskered gent answered the door. They inquired if he knew anywhere they could get accommodations for the night. He said, "You can stay here if you like. I can bed you, but can't grub you." It is very plain what he said, and everybody knew what he meant.

He turned the noun "grub" into a verb just as he had already done with "bed." The spoken language can't be outdone when it comes to creativity.

Dear Grammar Lady,
What is wrong with this sentence: "The guest book is in charge of Mary Jones?"

I think it's not the guest book that's in charge, but the other way around. "Mary Jones is in charge of the guest book" or maybe "The guest book is in the charge of Mary Jones."

Dear Grammar Lady,
What's with referring to children as "olds" and "graders"? My ten-year-old—what is an old? The fifth graders went to the zoo. Are they too lazy to add "child?"

I must admit I never thought of that.

Dear Grammar Lady,
Why do we use the expression "take a shower"? We don't go anywhere with it?

That's just the way we express the idea in English, using the verb "take." There are lots of expressions like it—take a test, take a break. They aren't logical, but English seldom is.

Dear Grammar Lady,
Can you help me fix this sentence? "They referred a woman with a broken exhaust pipe and three flat tires."

I suspect it was the woman's vehicle that had the problems and not the woman herself. How about: A woman whose car had a broken exhaust pipe and . . . was referred?

Dear Grammar Lady,
I don't like the use of extra prepositions. For example, "listen up" has become popular. I have always shuddered when someone says, "Where's it at?" My grammar teacher (over fifty years ago) would reply, "It's before the at."

I concur. One of my daughter's teachers always says "Serious up!" It drives the kids crazy.

Dear Grammar Lady,
Is "overtyped" a word, as in "I made a mistake, but I overtyped it."

I can't find it in any of the references; use the two-word verb "typed over." When "over" comes before words like typed, *it means in excess: overdone; overbooked; overrun. "Overtyped" would have a meaning different from the one you want.*

Dear Grammar Lady,
Can you help me with the right word? A committee I'm forming

needs to have qualified people of both sexes. Should I say "a qualified bisexual committee"?

The first meaning of bisexual is "of men and women," but your phrase as worded could have more than one meaning. Why not say "a committee of qualified women and men"?

Dear Grammar Lady,
Here is a headline from a local paper: "Kinks are being found in (local school's) armor." I believe the writer meant to say "chinks." It must be an unknown word, because it appears again in the story as kinks.

Perhaps the writer was afraid using the correct expression might constitute an ethnic slur.

Dear Grammar Lady,
In recent years many public speakers have zeroed in on their particular platform or point by saying "but more importantly . . ." Is this a fault of grammar? I never thought of important as an adverb, but as an adjective. For example: "but what is more important . . ." If the use of "importantly" is, indeed, incorrect, your column will be a great boon to many a public speaker.

It is my fervent hope that "importantly" will prove to be a verbal fad and not become an adverb preceding a sentence as the dreaded "hopefully" seems to be doing. Thank you for the kind words, but I fear this column will have little effect on public speakers who use such constructions.

❊**Goofy Goof:** A radio announcer, congratulating a woman on being one hundred years old, called her the day's centurion.

Dear Grammar Lady,
If we make "tantrum" into a verb, is the final *m* doubled before adding "ing?"

Why on earth would you want to make this into a verb? The phrase "to have/having a tantrum" has a very respectable history and is quite descriptive. However, jargon is irresistible for some fields; so here's the answer. No—the final consonant is doubled only if the stress is on the last syllable in two-syllable words (occur/occurring). In "tantrum" the stress is on the first syllable.

Dear Grammar Lady,
When did the verb "share" replace "tell someone something"? I don't like to hear someone thank me for "sharing a piece of information." I can share my seat on the bus or my piece of cake, but I tell or give someone information.

It may have come up with children "sharing" during grade school "show and tell," but I agree that it sounds rather childish.

Dear Grammar Lady,
How is the word spelled that sounds like "nash," and means to grind one's teeth.

It's gnash. There aren't very many English words that start with the combination gn. *Some of the more common ones are gnarl, gnat, gnaw, gnome, and gnu. The g was originally pronounced, but was lost over the years, leaving people who complain about our eccentric spelling with one more piece of ammunition.*

Dear Grammar Lady,
I wish you would address the use of "bad" words. As a former school nurse, I used to hear every day in casual conversation the "f" word. It was used to say hello: "How the . . . are you?" The students did not consider this a "bad" word. Are there any bad words today?

There are six or seven words that are not permitted on the public airways, but I'm not exactly sure which ones they are because we seem to hear everything.

Dear Grammar Lady,
During a football game recently there was the announcement of "the untimely death" of a famous sports figure. My question is when does the death of another human being become "timely"? Please clarify this matter before I die of an untimely/timely death.

I hope we can provide a timely response and prevent any kind of demise. The words timely *and* untimely *refer to the appropriateness in time of the noun that follows. The phrase "untimely death" has become a familiar one when a (relatively) young person dies, but of course there is no use of such a phrase when someone of advanced years dies.*

Dear Grammar Lady,
One common error—although possibly not an error in grammar—is using "you" when "I" is correct. For example, a person might say "I like to start the day with a thirty-minute jog; it makes you feel better all day." His jogging doesn't make me feel better. Why doesn't he say "It makes me feel better"?

The use of "you" to refer to people in general is very common in speech, but it can be confusing when interpreted as referring to an individual as in the reader's example. Very formal styles of speech would use "one." "Jogging makes one feel better."

Dear Grammar Lady,
I know that a "donee" is "one who receives or is given to" and a "payee" is "one who is paid," but I am distressed by the use of such coined words as "escapee." One who is escaped?! I've seen "standee," "attendee," and other such monstrosities.

The analogy with employer/employee does seem to have gotten out of hand. What would be the difference between an escaper and an escapee based on this analogy? Stander/standee? Attender/attendee?

Dear Grammar Lady,
I am not a native speaker of English, but there seems to be a mistake in this recipe. It says to "peel and core" the apples for the pie. If we take the peel off and take out the core, shouldn't it be "unpeel" and "uncore" the apples.

Logically it certainly should. Logic, however, has little to do with language use. Questions like this make us think about our language, and I marvel that anyone ever learns it.

Dear Grammar Lady,
Why do they call it an "ambulance" when it doesn't walk?

The original French phrase was "hôpital ambulant" (walking hospital) meaning a field hospital that "walked" among the wounded. The French adjective became a noun in English.

Dear Grammar Lady,
How do you spell a special kind of hit that kids give each other—nuggie?

The first spelling is noogie (oo as in book), but nuggie and nugie are also acceptable according to the unabridged dictionary. It's defined as a light jab to the head, back, or upper arm accompanied by a twisting motion of the curled up second or third knuckle, which is apparently the source for the word. It's done as a gesture of affection or painfully as a prank. The teenage girl at our house claims it's some pointless thing that boys do to each other.

Dear Grammar Lady,
I found an item describing a college professor who has set up a language institute, "a program involving six languages which she created and organized."

Comment: It's fairly unusual for a person to create even one language, but six?

Dear Grammar Lady,
Your recent item about using nouns as verbs reminds me of a bit of conversation I overheard at a lunch counter. One waitress was about to go on her lunch break, and said to her replacement, "All these customers have been watered, but none have been desserted." Waitress—uh, waitperson—ese?

That's great. The politically correct term would probably be "waiterese" or "waitstaffers."

Dear Grammar Lady,
Political correctness is going a bit too far these days. I heard

a woman describing "nonpeople of color" and spent the next several hours trying to decide what she meant.

The possibilities are endless; nonpeople includes everything but people. How about purple trees? I agree that efforts to avoid giving offense regarding differences have come to the point of interfering with communication. It's time to be a little less paranoid and a little more sensible.

Dear Grammar Lady,
The sportscaster and the weatherman on a local station were discussing a heart "rendering" story.

The image is a good one if you think of the meaning of "render" as processing for industrial use, i.e., rendering animal carcasses. "Render" usually means "to cause to be": the rude comment rendered him speechless. The verb they wanted was "rend," to split by force, a heart-rending story.

Dear Grammar Lady,
How can someone be "legally drunk"? If you are drunk and driving it is "illegal." If you are drunk at home and do not drive, isn't that "legally" drunk?

Interesting question, but I think it means "drunk according to the law." But you're right, it seems like an oxymoron.

Dear Grammar Lady,
OK I confess. In my first letter I addressed you as the GrammEr Lady. I was going to write others such as the Grammor Lady and Grammur Lady, etc. I got the idea from a sporting good store. They put a sign in their window—WORMS FOR SALE. Nobody paid much attention, but then he changed it to WERMS

FOR SALE, then WIRMS, and last WURMS FOR SALE. Needless to say, he received much publicity from this.

I probably didn't notice Grammer, because so many people spell it that way and are not being funny. The similar pronunciation of er/ir/ur/or shows one major problem for people learning English. Thanks for the laugh.

Dear Grammar Lady,
We have all heard that "a preposition is not a proper part of speech to end a sentence with." I offer the following question, which a little boy asked his father who, having told his son he would read to him after supper, brought a book into the boy's upstairs bedroom. "Why did you bring that book which I did not want to be read to out of after up for?"

Quite a precocious kid.

Dear Grammar Lady,
I'd like to comment on something I'm hearing fairly often these days. It reminds me of the "I could care less" phenomenon, in that the speaker is saying the opposite of what he/she means. Someone will say in parting with a dear one, "I'll miss not seeing you," when they mean "I'll miss seeing you" and they don't even realize it.

Now that you mention it, I have heard this one.

Dear Grammar Lady,
If someone finds "a body," can it be anything other than

✳ **Goofy Goof:** At a Santa Fe gas station: We will sell gasoline to anyone in a glass container.

"dead"? There was a newscast about someone finding two "dead bodies." It seemed odd.

You're right, "live bodies" are not discovered.

Dear Grammar Lady,
I recently saw this sign. WE HAVE DOUGLAS FURS AND FRAZIER FURS. This might be a site for the animal rights activists to picket.

Or at least the correct-spelling police.

Dear Grammar Lady,
Here is my contribution to the search for a gender-neutral third-person singular pronoun. You recently pointed out that s/he works in writing but not in speech. I would suggest that it be pronounced "shahee." As for him/her and his/hers, I offer "hrim" (huh-rim) and "hris" (huh-ris). In spelling, the feminine is shoehorned in like a reinserted rib. In pronunciation, the "her" is heard first. Politically, that should balance. Another possibility would be to use "it" to refer to all people.

The last suggestion might be the most sensible; there are lots of languages where there are no gender distinctions in the third singular.

Dear Grammar Lady,
You asked for examples of absurd politically correct language. How about that idiotic Ms (??) business? Most women desperately try to add a Mrs. to their name.

I fear that attitudes like this were what got us into the trouble to begin with.

Dear Grammar Lady,
Is there a common use of "service" as a verb? Something like
"the waiter will service your table"?

*Not that I know. You can have your car serviced, and in an-
imal husbandry females are commonly serviced by males; but
I've never had my table "serviced" by a waiter.*

Chapter Thirteen

If in Doubt, Check These Out

I use a lot of reference works to make sure I give accurate information. Sometimes the authorized sources disagree. When that happens, I give my best advice.

Aaron, Jane E. *The Essential Handbook for Writers*. 2nd ed. New York: HarperCollins, 1997. This is a must for people who write papers and need bibliographic references. It has complete reference citations for MLA, APA, *Chicago Manual*, and CBE styles, including Internet and Web sites. It is mainly meant for a college audience and has some English as a second language tips.

Agee, Jon. *So Many Dynamos! and Other Palindromes*. New York: Farrar, Straus & Giroux, 1994. The palindromes are illustrated by very clever cartoons.

The Associated Press Stylebook and Libel Manual. 6th ed. Reading, MA: Addison-Wesley, 1996.

Bruder, Mary Newton, and Elaine Williams. *Cracking the Code: Learning to Read and Write in English*. Pittsburgh: University of Pittsburgh Press for the English Language Institute, 1986. This book is the basis for teaching reading by combining phonics and sight-words. It's rather good, if I do say so myself. (Note the author credit.)

The Compact Edition of the Oxford English Dictionary, Oxford, England: Oxford University Press, 1971. The OED, as it is familiarly called, is a multivolume dictionary that includes the history of English from the earliest days. The version I have requires a magnifying glass as well as eyeglasses and strong light to read.

Crystal, David. *The Cambridge Encyclopedia of the English Language*. Cambridge, England: Cambridge University Press, 1995. A wonderful compendium of facts about the history of English, well illustrated.

Dickson, Paul. *Labels for Locals: What to Call People from Abilene to Zimbabwe*. Springfield, MA: Merriam-Webster, 1997.

Grambs, David. *Death by Spelling: A Compendium of Tests, Super Tests and Killer Bees*. New York: Harper & Row, 1989. This is an amusing look at English spelling, historic and current. Words are grouped according to certain spelling principles and accompanied by short texts followed by spelling tests of various types. The second half includes words grouped by college course types: Anatomy, anthropology, archaeology. There is no reason, however, that the book could not be used by high school students or other adults who want to beef up their spelling.

Greenbaum, Sidney, and Whitcut, Janet. *Guide to English Usage*. Harlow, England: Longman, 1988. This usage book in dictionary form discusses American and British usage.

Grossman, Ellie. *The Grammatically Correct Handbook*. New York: Hyperion, 1997.

Kilpatrick, James J. *Fine Print: Reflections on the Writing Art*. Kansas City, MO: Andrews and McMeel, 1993. This readable volume has four chapters of advice for writers, one on reference works, and a dictionary-order usage chapter.

Lederer, Richard. *Crazy English*. New York: Pocket Books, 1998.

Manser, Martin. *The Guinness Book of Words*. London: Guinness

Books, 1988. This book is full of word games and little-known facts about English words.

Morris, William and Mary. *Dictionary of Word and Phrase Origins.* 2nd ed. New York: Harper & Row, 1977. I use this dictionary first when someone wants to know where a word came from.

The New York Public Library Desk Reference. New York: Simon & Schuster, Webster's New World, 1989. When people ask off-the-wall questions that may not have anything to do with English, this is the source I use.

O'Conner, Patricia T. *Woe Is I.* New York: Grosset/Putnam, 1996.

The Professional's Secretary's Handbook. Boston: Houghton Mifflin, 1984.

Quirk, Randolph, and Greenbaum, Sidney. *A Concise Grammar of Contemporary English.* New York: Harcourt Brace Jovanovich, 1973. This is a grammar text for linguistically oriented users.

The Random House Dictionary of the English Language. 2nd ed., unabridged. New York: Random House, 1987.

Roget's College Thesaurus in Dictionary Form. New York: Signet Books, 1985. A regular thesaurus is very difficult for beginners to use because of the layout of the topics. The dictionary form makes it easier and encourages people to look up new words.

Spears, Richard A. *Dictionary of American Slang and Colloquial Expressions.* Lincolnwood, IL: National Textbook Company, 1993. Someone called to ask the exact wording for the 1960s phrase "Turn on, tune in, and drop out." He was making an ad for TV and thought the phrase would be catchy.

Tillit, Bruce, and Mary Newton Bruder. *Speaking Naturally: Communication Skills in American English.* Cambridge, England: Cambridge University Press, 1984. This English as a second language text presents the different speaking styles for international students. And yes, that's me again as the coauthor.

Warriner, John. E., and Griffith, Francis. Warriner, *English Grammar and Composition.* Complete Course. Orlando: Harcourt Brace

Jovanovich, 1977. This is a compilation of the year-by-year course books that have been used in schools for many years. A very basic grammar text with a lot of examples and exercises. There is no answer key, but the exercises relate directly to the text, so it's easy to know if the answers are right.

Webster's Guide to Abbreviations. Springfield, MA: Merriam-Webster, 1985.

The Westminster Study Edition of THE HOLY BIBLE. Philadelphia: The Westminster Press, 1958.

A Brief Glossary of Grammar

active voice Writing or speech in which the subject performs the action in a sentence. *Jane loves the movie. Tom throws the rock.* See also **passive voice**.

adjective A word that modifies a noun, a pronoun, or another adjective. *The* persistent *man called me again.*

adverb A word that modifies a verb, an adjective, or another adverb. *The party was* terribly *boring.* Terribly is an adverb modifying the adjective, boring.

agreement Standard English grammar convention that the parts of a sentence should agree with each other in number. In the sentence *Mary has a cold,* the singular subject *Mary* is in agreement with the singular form of the verb *to have.*

antecedent The noun in a sentence to which a pronoun refers. Pronouns should agree with their antecedents in person, number, and gender. *She is the teacher who went home early. She* is the antecedent of *who. The new car has its own stereo system. Car* is the antecedent of *its.*

apostrophe Punctuation mark to indicate a missing letter (*It's on Saturday*) or to form a possessive (*Billy's dog broke the leash*).

Possessives of pronouns like *theirs* and *its* do not use an apostrophe.

article *A, an,* and *the.*

cc Abbreviation for carbon copy; used to indicate that a copy of a letter has been sent to another person. Courtesy copy seems more fitting now that carbon copies are outmoded.

clause A group of related words that contains a subject and a verb. Clauses may be either dependent (cannot stand alone as a sentence)—*Although she had enough money*—or independent (can stand alone as a sentence)—*she didn't have a ticket.*

collective noun A singular noun that refers to a group of persons, places, or things, such as *team, group, class, workforce,* and so on.

colloquial language Informal, conversational style of speech. See **informal language**.

complement, or object complement In the common grammatical pattern Subject + Verb + Object + Complement, the complement refers to the object. The grammatical mistake often made is to use an adverb, as in *Chop the onion thinly,* when the adjective, *Chop the onion thin,* is the correct complement to onion. *Thinly chop the onion,* in which the adverb *thinly* refers to the verb *chop,* is a different onion altogether.

complement, or subject complement In the pattern Subject + Be/Linking verb + Adjective/noun, the complement refers to the subject and must be the same kind of word that goes in the subject slot. This pattern results in the formal pattern *It is I* that some find difficult. It is also the reason that linking verbs (feel, taste, look, seem, sound, and smell) require adjectives after them—*The milk tastes bad; the music sounds terrible; I feel bad about the accident.*

complex sentence A sentence made up of one dependent clause and one independent clause. *Although she had the money, she didn't have a ticket.*

compound noun A noun made up of more than one word; the meaning of the new word is different from the individual original words: copycat; baseball; White House. The intonation of compound words is different from an adjective + noun sequence. If you say "the white house," and "the White House" aloud, you'll hear the difference.

compound sentence A sentence made up of two independent clauses. *We liked the way the VW Bug handled; the next day we bought it.*

conditional Sentences that have a clause with *if* and describe cause and possible result. *If it rains, we'll cancel the picnic. If it had snowed, they would have closed the roads.*

conjunction Words such as *and, but, or, nor, since, unless, however,* and so on, that connect groups of related words in sentences.

consonant A speech sound made by constriction on the speech mechanism. Consonants include *b, c, d, f, g, h, j, k, l, m, n, p, q, r, s, t, v, w, x, y, z.*

consultative language style A language style used to gain information from strangers. It is characterized by careful pronunciation and correct grammar and polite ending remarks. (I can't resist. A woman from a bank asked to leave a message for my husband. There was a pause. Then she asked, "Can you write down the message?" I retorted, "I am perfectly capable of writing it down if you will tell me what it is." She needs to upgrade her consultative lingo.)

count noun Items that can be counted and take a plural ending. One pencil, two pencils; one child, two children.

dangling modifier, or dangling participle A grammar goof in which there is an unclear referent for a modifier, such as a participial phrase. *Smothered in ketchup, Bill ate the French fries.*

dependent clause A group of related words that includes a subject and a verb, but cannot stand alone as a complete sentence. *When we were very young* is a dependent clause.

dialect The sound and vocabulary used by people in a certain area of the country. Usually, this refers to regional dialects, such as those heard in Boston, the South, or Canada.

direct object The person, place, or thing that is acted upon by the verb in a sentence. *I washed the car.* The word *car* is the direct object. See also **indirect object**.

eponym The brand name of an item used as the common name of the product or its use—Kleenex for tissue of any type; Xerox used as a verb to make copies.

formal language style The language style used when people are on their best language behavior—in the pulpit, in the academic lecture, the company boardroom. It is characterized by long complete sentences and Latinate and Greek vocabulary.

hypercorrection The creation of a grammar mistake because of misunderstanding of the general rule. *Between you and I* instead of the correct *between you and me* seems to be a case of hypercorrection.

independent clause A group of related words that includes a subject and a verb and that can stand as a complete sentence. *I am going to take a walk, whether or not it rains.* The part of this sentence before the comma is an independent clause. See **clause.**

indirect object The person, place, or thing that is the recipient of the action of a verb like *to give. Delilah gave Samson a haircut.* Samson is the indirect object. Haircut is the direct object. See also **direct object**.

infinitive Form of a verb used with the word *to*, as in to eat, to drink, to sleep, or perchance to dream.

informal language style The language used between close colleagues and friends. It is characterized by shortened words—gonna, gotta, waitin'.

intimate language style The language used within a family. It is characterized by the lack of lead-ins to topics, and the continuation of the same conversation over long periods of time.

irregular verbs Verbs that must be memorized for the past and participle forms—go/went/gone, shrink/shrank/shrunk.

linking verbs Verbs that link what comes after to what went before. They are verbs of the senses—look, taste, sound, smell, feel, seem. These verbs require adjectives to follow because there is a noun or pronoun in the subject and adjectives modify nouns.

mass noun A noun that isn't normally counted—milk, news, homework, so there is no plural form unless a phrase is added—two cartons of milk.

metaphor A comparison that doesn't use the words *like* or *as. My love is a red, red rose.*

noncount noun See **mass noun.**

nonrestrictive phrase Material that is not essential to the identification of a noun in a sentence and therefore is set off by commas. *Mr. Jones, formerly with XYZ Corp., has taken a new position with ABC.*

nonstandard Language use characterized by consistent errors in subject-verb agreement (*he don't . . .*), double negatives (*I'm not no fashion expert*) and problems with irregular past participles (*he had went*).

noun A word for a person, place, or thing. See **count noun, mass noun, collective noun.**

object Word or group of words that is affected directly by the action of the verb. *I tore the dress.* The noun *dress* is the object in this sentence. See **direct and indirect objects.**

oxymoron A phrase that seemingly contradicts itself. *The icy fire of passion.*

parallel structure A rule for writing that similar ideas should be expressed in a similar way. For example, using the-*ing* form of a verb to begin each item in a list is parallel structure.

participle A verb form, ending in -*ing* that can be used as an adjective or a verb. Verb: *I am writing to inform you.* Adjective: *The writing instructor is talented.* Verb: *I have written the letter.* Adj.: *The written word is different from the spoken.*

passive voice The opposite of active voice. In passive voice, the subject is acted upon, as in, *The rock is thrown by Tom.* The active voice version would be *Tom throws the rock.* The Grammar Lady normally eschews the passive because it is less direct and generally harder to process in reading.

phatic language Language used for social purposes to start, continue, or finish conversations. *Hello, Goodbye! Nice weather we're having.*

phrase A group of connected words. Noun phrase—*the little boy.* Verb phrase—*saw the snake.* Prepositional phrase—*in the house.*

predicate The part of the sentence that includes the verb and its modifiers and objects. In *The quick brown fox jumped over the lazy dog,* "jumped over the lazy dog" is the predicate. See **subject.**

predicate nominative Another term for subject complement. See **complement.**

prefix Addition of elements to the beginning of a word to change the meaning. Un + necessary, dis + bar, re + apply.

preposition A word that shows the relation between its object and some other word in the sentence, such as *at, in, on, by, down, from, off, out, through, to, up, of, for,* and *with.*

pronoun A word that takes the place of a noun, such as *I, me, you, he, him, she, her, they, them, who, what,* and *that.*

redundant Unnecessary repetition of words—*free gift, close proximity, return back.*

reflexive pronoun Pronouns ending in -*self* or -*selves* and referring to someone mentioned previously or anticipated in the sentence, turning the action back on the subject of the sentence. *I* *asked the question myself* (previous). *On behalf of the board and myself, I* . . . (anticipated).

regionalism Language element found mostly in one area of the country. *Wait on someone* in the South is usually *wait for someone* in most parts of the country. The words *soda* and *pop* are discussed endlessly on college campuses where students from different regions meet.

restrictive clause A clause containing information that is essential to the identification of a noun in a sentence and therefore should not be set off by commas. *The man who called wanted to know about commas.*

sentence fragment A group of words that does not form a complete thought with both a subject and verb.

simile A comparison using the word *like* or *as*. *It was like a whole new world. Her eyes were as big as saucers.*

slang Nonstandard language used mostly by teens and special groups who don't want their language understood.

sociolinguistics The study of language in its social context. The discussion of the appropriate style of language use in different situations is an example of sociolinguistics in action.

split infinitive Refers to the placement of a word after the *to* in the verb form, as in *to boldly go where* . . . Grammar purists like to avoid splitting infinitives at all costs, though it is no longer thought to be a high crime so much as a misdemeanor.

subject The words in a sentence that represent the person, place, thing, or idea that the sentence is about. In *The quick brown fox jumped over the lazy dog,* the *quick brown fox* is the subject. See **predicate.**

subjunctive Expresses a wish, command, or condition that is contrary to fact, such as *If I were you, I would go home now.*

suffix Elements of language added to the end of a word to change the part of speech or other grammatical function. Reach + ed = past tense; eventual (adj) + ly = adverb.

tense The time of the action of a verb, such as present tense, past tense, future tense.

thesaurus A reference book organized by words to find synonyms and antonyms. *Roget's Thesaurus* is the most famous thesaurus for English.

verb The part of a sentence that expresses action. Jane *smiled*.

vowel The letters *a, e, i, o, u,* and *y* and *w* when they are at the end of a word or syllable—very, wow. (The first w is a consonant; the second is a vowel.)

Irregular Verbs

The verbs are organized in alphabetical order to facilitate use. If there are two correct forms, the most common one is listed first. If there is a specialized use, examples are given.

Present	Past	Perfect	Present	Past	Perfect
am/is	was	been	arise	arose	arisen
awake	awoke	awaken			
bear	bore	borne	beat	beat	beat/beaten
become	became	become	begin	began	begun
bend	bent	bent	beseech	beseeched	beseeched
bet	bet/betted	bet/betted	besought	besought	
bid (offer)	bid	bid	bid (invite)	bade	bidden
bind	bound	bound	bite	bit	bitten
bleed	bled	bled	blow	blew	blown
break	broke	broken	bring	brought	brought
build	built	built	buy	bought	bought
cast	cast	cast	catch	caught	caught
choose	chose	chosen	cleave	cleaved	cleaved/cloven

Present	Past	Perfect	Present	Past	Perfect
cling	clung	clung			
creep	crept	crept	cut	cut	cut
deal	dealt	dealt	dig	dug	dug
dive	dived dove	dived dove	do	did	done
draw	drew	drawn	dream	dreamed dreamt	dreamed dreamt
drink	drank	drunk			
drive	drove	driven	dwell	dwelt/ dwelled	Both
eat	ate	eaten			
fall	fell	fallen	feed	fed	fed
feel	felt	felt	find	found	found
fight	fought	fought	flee	fled	fled
fling	flung	flung	fly	flew	flown
forbid	forbade	forbidden	forego (precede)	forewent	foregone
forgo (give up)	forwent	forgone	forget	forgot	forgotten
forgive	forgave	forgiven	forsake	forsook	forsaken
freeze	froze	frozen			
get	got	gotten	give	gave	given
go	went	gone	grow	grew	grown
grind	ground	ground			
hang (suspend)	hung	hung	have	had	had
(Hang "to execute" is regular.)					
hear	heard	heard	hide	hid	hidden
hit	hit	hit	hold	held	held
hurt	hurt	hurt			
keep	kept	kept	kneel	kneeled knelt	kneeled knelt
know	knew	known			
lay (place)	laid	laid	lead	led	led
lean	leaned/ leant	Both	leap	leaped/ leapt	Both

Irregular Verbs

Present	Past	Perfect	Present	Past	Perfect
leave	left	left	lend	lent	lent
let	let	let	lie (recline)	lay	lain
			(Lie to "tell untruths" is regular.)		
light	lit/lighted	lit/lighted	lose	lost	lost
make	made	made	mean	meant	meant
meet	met	met	mistake	mistook	mistaken
mow	mowed	mowed/mown			
paid	paid		plead	pleaded/pled	pleaded/pled
prove	proved	proved/proven			
put	put	put			
quit	quit	quit			
read	read /red/	read /red/	rid	rid	rid
ride	rode	ridden	ring	rang	rung
rise	rose	risen	run	ran	run
say	said	said	see	saw	seen
seek	sought	sought	sell	sold	sold
send	sent	sent	set (place)	set	set
sew	sewed	sewn	shake	shook	shaken
shed	shed	shed	shine (stars)	shone	shone
			("Shine shoes" is regular.)		
shoe	shoed/shod	Both	shoot	shot	shot
show	showed	shown/showed	shrink	shrank	shrunk
shut	shut	shut	sink	sank	sunk
sing	sang	sung	sit	sat	sat
slay	slew	slain	sleep	slept	slept
slide	slid	slid	sling	slung	slung
slink	slunk	slunk	slit	slit	slit
sneak	sneaked/snuck	sneaked/snuck	sow	sowed	sown/sowed
			speak	spoke	spoken
speed	sped/speeded	sped/speeded	spend	spent	spent

[255]

Present	Past	Perfect	Present	Past	Perfect
			spin	spun	spun
spit	spit/spat	spit/spat	split	split	split
spread	spread	spread	spring	sprang/ sprung	sprung
stand	stood	stood	steal	stole	stolen
stick	stuck	stuck	sting	stung	stung
stink	stank/stunk	stunk	strew	strewed	strewn/ strewed
stride	strode	stridden	strike	struck	struck/ stricken
string	strung	strung	strive	strived/ strove	strived/ striven
swear	swore	sworn			
sweat	sweat	sweat	sweep	swept	swept
swell	swelled	swelled/ swollen	swim	swam	swum
swing	swung	swung			
take	took	taken	teach	taught	taught
tear	tore	torn	tell	told	told
think	thought	thought	throw	threw	thrown
thrust	thrust	thrust	tread	trod	trodden
understand	u—stood	u—stood	upset	upset	upset
wake	woke/ waked	woken/ waked	wear	wore	worn
			weave	wove/ weaved	woven/ weaved
			wed	wed/ wedded	wed/ wedded
			weep	wept	wept
wet	wetted/ wet	wetted/ wet			
win	won	won	wind	wound	wound
wring	wrung	wrung	write	wrote	written

Answers to Mary's Bee

First Quiz Answers

1. Light umbrella to protect from the sun.
   parasol

2. Device for showing changing patterns.
   kaleidoscope

3. Photographers who pursue famous people.
   paparazzi

4. Light golden horse with nearly white mane and tail.
   palomino

5. Harsh, unpleasant sound.
   cacophony

6. To fawn.
   kowtow

7. Dessert topping.
   meringue

8. Upholstered seat along a wall.
   banquette

9. Casino employee who collects and pays off debts.
   croupier

10. Bandage to stop bleeding.
    tourniquet

11. Club used by police.
    truncheon

12. Petty, trivial.
    picayune

13. Fit of rage or hysteria.
    conniption

14. Triangle with two equal sides.
    isosceles

15. System of writing for the blind.
    braille

16. Encoding.
    encryption

17. Ceremonial greeting in the Middle East.
    salaam

18. Confuse.
    discombobulate

19. Shaky, run down.
    rickety

20. A shape like the Washington Monument.
    obelisk

Second Quiz Answers

1. abundant

2. division

3. expensive

4. dilemma

5. hospital

6. perceive

7. precede

8. succeed

9. sponsor

10. souvenir

Third Quiz Answers

1. separate

2. embarrass

3. pronunciation

4. accommodate

5. occurrence

6. conscience

7. definitely

8. indispensable

9. dependent

10. nickel

Fourth Quiz Answers

1. Nut or fruit-filled candy.
   nougat

2. Mexican peppers.
   jalapeño

3. Clear soup.
   consommé

4. Ground vegetables fried in patties.
   falafel

5. Spicy Chinese cooking.
   Szechuan

6. Espresso with milk.
   cappuccino

7. Having a protein found in wheat flour.
   glutenous

8. Appetizers.
   hors d'oeuvres

9. Dish of beans and corn.
   succotash

10. Support for hot dish.
    trivet

11. Small cabbage-type vegetable.
    kohlrabi

12. Sugary brown syrup.
    molasses

13. Spice from tree bark.
    cinnamon

14. Type of turnip.
    rutabaga

15. Fermented cherry.
    maraschino

Fifth Quiz Answers

1. falsify

2. nicely

3. rudeness

4. policing

5. usable

6. useless

7. courageous

8. landscaping

9. ninety

10. sorely

Sixth Quiz Answers

1. forgetting

2. forgetful

3. canceled

4. preferring

5. preferable

6. propeller

7. benefited

8. inferring

9. reddest

10. interfering

Seventh Quiz Answers

1. To make liquid.
   liquefy

2. Foolish.
   asinine

3. Vivid reddish orange.
   vermilion

4. Soft leather shoe.
   moccasin

5. A treatment to establish immunity.
   inoculation

6. Adapt.
   accommodate

7. Sponsor of entertainment.
   impresario

8. Revive.
   resuscitate

9. Take the place of.
    supersede

10. Very ornate.
    rococo

11. A large tent.
    pavilion

12. Make rare, thin, or less dense.
    rarefy

13. White sandwich spread.
    mayonnaise

14. Accompanying musical part played by a single instru-
    ment.
    obbligato

15. Excite pleasurably.
    titillate

16. Dehydrate.
    desiccate

17. Violation of something sacred.
    sacrilegious

18. One who assumes an identity.
    impostor

19. Agreement in opinion.
    consensus

20. Tiny.
    minuscule

Perfectly Punctuated Quiz Answers

First Quiz Answers

Punctuation in parentheses ( ) is optional.

1. Where were you on Friday, October 13, 1985(,) at 10 o'clock in the morning?

2. The policy covers collision, liability, property damage(,) and personal injury.

3. Jane Morgan, Esq. will address the group this month.

4. You always seem to know what to do, Bill.

5. Introducing herself to all the guests, she made her way toward the door.

6. After you have completed the tape, please send it to my attention.

7. We will discuss this further when you have time. (No commas needed.)

8. Take as long as you need with this report, but we need it by the end of the day.

9. After conducting a national poll, the researchers concluded that the prices of bananas are too high in our area; and they have recommended that we should boycott all merchants who have bananas.

10. If you hear of a good new dictionary, please let me know.

Second Quiz Answers

Punctuation in parentheses ( ) is optional.

1. The man asked for coffee, toast(,) and ham and eggs.

2. New York, Maryland, Pennsylvania(,) and Ohio are in the same region.

3. The policy covers collision, liability, and property damage.

4. Apples, peaches, pears(,) and grapes are available now.

5. We fought, cried, laughed(,) and sang.

Third Quiz Answers

1. The man asked, "What's for dinner?"

2. "I hate this place!" yelled Jenny.

3. Where did you find that old tape of *I Love Lucy*?

4. The comic book store has a lot of old copies of *Super-man*.

5. *Macbeth, Hamlet, Othello,* and *Much Ado About Nothing* will be performed this year.

Answers to The Quizzical I

1. "If this was murder, I'm going to solve it," said the detective.
   was—not subjunctive (It's possible it was a murder.)

2. If she was angry about the broken vase, she didn't show it.
   was—not subjunctive (She could have been angry.)

3. It's very important that he earn enough money for tuition.
   earn—subjunctive (It is important.)

4. His voice rang out as if he were Laurence Olivier performing Shakespeare.
   were—subjunctive (He is not Laurence Olivier.)

5. I don't know if she was late or on time.
   was—not subjunctive (She could have been late.)

6. If the paint was wet, you'd get marks on your slacks.
   was—not subjunctive (The paint might be wet.)

7. I think she possesses the intelligence and ambition to succeed.
   possesses—not subjunctive (Think does not require subjunctive.)

8. I wish it were the 1980s again.
   were—subjunctive (It's not the 1980s.)

9. It's necessary that the company provide the information.
   provide—subjunctive (It's necessary.)

10. If the political climate wasn't such a mess, we'd all be a lot happier.
    wasn't—not subjunctive (It is a mess.)

Second Quiz Answers

1. We have chosen the new captain.

2. He has seen the award-winning movie.

3. Have you ridden in the new buses?

4. They have come late for every performance.

5. Has she given him the present?

6. I have begun a new exercise program.

7. Have you done the crossword puzzle?

8. The new car has broken down three times in three weeks.

9. They haven't spoken to her for years.

10. You've torn the book.

Third Quiz Answers

1. We inferred from his remarks that he was a friend of the family.

2. She implied that she could have us fired.

3. The police inferred from the sequence of events how the accident had happened.

4. Did she infer their body language correctly?

5. Did he mean to imply that I was lying?

6. I inferred from the look on her face that she was very angry.

7. They implied that they were going to bid on the house themselves.

8. Did you infer the same message as I got from his speech?

Fourth Quiz Answers

1. Pittsburgh lies at the head of the Ohio River.
   lie

2. She laid the rumor to rest at last.
   lay

3. Did you lay the papers where he can find them?
   lay

4. The leaves have lain in their yard for months.
   lie

5. The workers have laid the foundation for the new terminal.
   lay

6. She lay down for a rest before the children came home.
   lie

7. The empty trash cans have been lying at the curb for days.
   lie

8. When will they be laying the floor?
   lay

9. He had the habit of lying in a hammock on Sunday afternoons.
   lie

10. She laid the baby next to the puppy for the photograph.
    lay

Index

Index